MW01017161

Follow Me

Meditations on the Passion of Jesus

Follow Me

Meditations on the Passion of Jesus

Bertha Catherine Madott

NOVALIS

Follow Me: Meditations on the Passion of Jesus
    is published by Novalis.

Cover design and layout: Gilles Lepine

Artwork: Nina Price

© 1994, Novalis, St. Paul University, Ottawa, Canada

Business Office: Novalis, 49 Front St. East, 2nd Floor,
    Toronto, Ontario, M5E 1B3

Editorial Office: Novalis, 223 Main Street,
    Ottawa, Ontario, K1S 1C4

Legal deposit: 3rd trimester, 1994
    National Library of Canada
    Bibliothèque nationale du Québec

Printed in Canada.

Canadian Cataloguing in Publication Data

Madott, Bertha Catherine, 1948-

    Follow me: meditations on Jesus' Passion

ISBN 2-89088-682-4

    1. Jesus Christ – Passion – Meditations.

I. Title.

BT306.4.M34 1994   232.96   C94-900789-7

NOVALIS

With thanks to
James Wells, OFM,
Roger Bonneau, O. Carm,
and Leonard Broughan, O. Carm,
for their insight and inspiration;
to the Granata family in Italy
for their generous hospitality;
and, especially, to my mother,
Georgina Madott,
for her unfailing encouragement and enthusiasm.
For all my family and friends,
with gratitude.

Table of Contents

---

* Denotes one of the traditional *Seven last words of Christ*.

Prologue

Many centuries ago, a group of friends gathered together in the heart of the old city of Jerusalem; we can imagine them seated in an upper room, the prep-arations for their long happy Passover meal spread out on the table before them. They intended to celebrate this feast as their ancestors had before them, remembering Israel's passage from the death of slavery in Egypt to the freedom of life in the Promised Land. To their surprise, this year's supper touched them in unexpected ways; after reciting the tradi-tional psalms, they watched their leader offer a blessing of unusually solemn intent. His words left them strangely moved; their simple meal, the bread, the wine, satisfied more than mere physical hunger. But soon afterward, something happened; the mood of the evening changed. Instead of continuing to sit together, telling stories of the past and sharing hopes for the future, they found themselves outdoors in the darkened city, walking slowly in the direction of the Mount of Olives. This was not how they expected the evening to end.

1

The agony in the garden

Mark 14:32-42[1]

The long journey to Calvary begins in a garden on a hillside. Imagine a warm spring evening with storm clouds gathering in the sky at dusk; if I look thoughtfully with my mind's eye, I can see them. There is tension in the air, the electricity of a humid night before a thunderstorm when everything in the atmosphere vibrates with anticipation and anxiety. For days now it has been impossible for Jesus to ignore the growing hostility of those in command. Like storm clouds that promise a night of unsettled rest, vague hints and warnings cast a darkening shadow over his words at the Passover gathering in Jerusalem.

On that night many hundreds of years ago, this growing uneasiness finally drove Jesus away from the supper table and up to the Mount of Olives; they say

---

[1] The source of each meditation is found in the words and images of the Gospel narratives. At the beginning of each chapter, there is a reference to a specific passage in Scripture.

that the garden there was one of his favourite places to pray. No intelligent and sensitive onlooker could fail to recognize the destructive forces that were lying in wait, massing together like black and ominous clouds, and Jesus was most definitely a person of intelligence and sensitivity. It is no wonder that fear and anxiety were with him when he walked into the garden to pray.

There is a time when prayer transfigures us with radiant happiness and tranquility; a time when every physical cell and spiritual impulse join together in one shattering leap of joy and thanksgiving. And then there is prayer that has a different origin, that speaks from other powerful human needs: prayer that shakes every bone and muscle like a body trembling from some dangerous tropical fever; prayer that is wrenched out like a stubborn tree root long buried in hard and unforgiving ground. These are the prayers that belong to our darkest and most harrowing nights. We need to remind ourselves that Jesus likewise shared in all human life, for only then can we see him suffering and praying in this way, suffering and praying just as we do.

I cannot imagine Jesus as he is so often portrayed: kneeling at a rock, long chestnut hair illuminated by the ghastly glow of an artificial halo, in silent contemplation of a lurid chalice. But I can see him pacing in the darkness, stopping a moment to rest against the side of a hill, shaking his head, not yet ready to believe that his life's work has brought him here to this, not yet able to accept all that will be waiting at the hands of those who have not understood his message. And I can see him sweat: a sweat born of the same fear and anxiety that plague us in our moments of confusion and turmoil. I strain to hear the prayer that escapes his lips, to appreciate all that his struggle should mean to me, but sometimes all I hear is silence.

In sadness, I admit to myself that after a while it takes too much effort to watch with him, this truly blameless person, whose message has been one of peace, love and forgiveness, whose every word and action hold out the promise of hope. I get tired, distracted, bored; my own problems, big and small, stand in the way of my concentration. The surroundings of my room, the noise from the street outside, all these little things affect me; then I think of the actions of his life and suddenly I am ashamed. He has deserved better from all of us than this.

Most of the time we leave Jesus there in the garden while we go about our daily business; we leave him trapped behind the stilted words of our traditional prayers and the artificial colours of our religious paintings, expressions of faith that belong in libraries and museums but not to the everyday world of life and imagination. Perhaps we ignore him because we are still asleep; with the disciples, we are in excellent company. Jesus still comes looking for us, waking us up gently, with good-natured laughter in his eyes as he sees us overcome by indifference and fatigue. And if we continue to sleep, he will keep coming back until finally we are ready to see him face the mystery of his last days.

> Lord, I don't always have the courage to look at you as a real human being who could suffer and laugh and bleed and sing, just as I can. It is too easy to hide the reality of your life behind the big words of theology; it is difficult to imagine you as one of us in all things except sin. Help me to watch a little with you during the events of your last days.

2

Judas

Matthew 26:47-50; 27:3-10

Many traditional representations of the Last Supper show a group of dignified and beautifully robed older men, artistically arranged along one side of a long table so that the painter can fit everyone neatly into the picture. Here are Jesus and his apostles, everyone blessed with pious looks and beatific smiles. All except for one man, for somewhere in the composition lurks a sinister and unattractive figure, clutching a purse to his treacherous bosom and looking furtively over his shoulder. This is supposed to be Judas.

It is often said that villains are especially interesting to study because of the ways in which they combine all the good and bad of humanity into one larger-than-life character. The portrait of Judas, however, is always drawn with uncompromising hard lines; there are no shifting shadows and soft edges to round out the corners of his personality. This artificial and one-sided perspective is vaguely unsatisfying; something about this tradition does not ring true to our experience of life.

When Jesus first began his public ministry, he gathered round him followers who had something of value to offer the group: energy, intelligence, loyalty, even charm and wit. He didn't single Judas out from the crowd merely because he was looking for a bad character who would be useful later on; likewise, Judas didn't follow Jesus down an unknown road, giving up his previous life and work, in the hope that some profitable mischief might come his way. We have to believe that Judas really was one of the Twelve in spirit, lifestyle and outlook; he knew and understood Jesus' work and message.

Similarly, if Judas was responsible for the common purse, as John's Gospel suggests, this in itself wouldn't make him the money-grubbing enemy of humanity; perhaps Judas merely had a good head for business, a little more education, a great deal of common sense. And regardless of what the religious painters have been telling us for centuries, none of these Apostles were old and venerable; they were strong and healthy, in the prime of life. They worked at jobs that required strength and stamina; they could easily have been well-built and handsome, just like their leader. The crowds were not drawn to Jesus and his friends simply because they walked around bathed in the glow of superhuman goodness: Jesus and his followers presented their message in a way that should also be described as "attractive."

So instead of the traditional figure of Judas as shifty-eyed traitor, imagine a clever and engaging man in his thirties, one of a close-knit group of friends who had a vision of the meaning of life that was impossible to resist. Imagine him listening intently to dozens of parables, told with authority and conviction by a Teacher whose words seemed to open up endless possibilities for change and fulfilment. Imagine Judas, like the others, in awe of both the power and the gentleness of their master, a Lord who was obeyed by the waves of the sea, but who still loved to play with little children. Imagine him watching the miracles, a witness to Jesus' concern for the well-being of the ordinary people of his time. Then imagine that something went wrong.

Within each of us there exists a confusing web of contradictions; if we are honest with ourselves, we recognize that sometimes our actions do not stem from clearly articulated and well-defined motives. Like the iridescent feathers on some exotic tropical bird, our colours change in the changing shadow and light; we are never the same from moment to moment, even in the way we see ourselves. There are shades of meaning and layers of understanding subtly woven through everything we do and everything we think. Given the limitations of human power, could the "pure, unadulterated evil" that is traditionally ascribed to Judas exist? When the moment came for their final confrontation in the garden, Jesus still addressed Judas as "friend" as the soldiers stood nearby, swords and clubs ready. Whatever led Judas to his tragic involvement with Jesus' enemies—fear of the power of the established order; greed for material goods; pride in his superior judgement; or even plain, old insanity—his story is but one more example of the mysteries that lie concealed and poorly understood within every human person.

Lord, I can hardly make sense of myself some days; one moment there is peace and harmony reigning within, the next is wrought with anxiety and confusion. Help me not just to understand but also to accept my humanity, however difficult it is for me to sort through my human strengths and weaknesses.

The crowd comes for Jesus

John 18:3-11

It is not a pleasant thing to be a soldier in an army of occupation. There is constant danger of sabotage and guerilla attacks; one may be living far from home in strange and hostile territory; the pay is terrible, the living conditions worse. Furthermore, if one is injured in the days before antibiotics and sterile surgical methods, one has to trust to luck, not medicine, in order to survive. The lessons of brutality are easily learned in this world: the necessity for quick and decisive action; sneering contempt for those who are not quick with their fists; the reluctance to accept any but one's comrades as trustworthy friends. In John's Gospel, Roman soldiers take part in the confrontation with Jesus at Gethsemane. Regardless of the exact composition of the crowd—soldiers, rowdies, Temple police, professional trouble-makers, indignant locals—it could not have been a reassuring encounter.

All of us have trouble remembering that Jesus did not want to die; we forget the horror he felt during his insights in the garden of Gethsemane. It is rarely easy for us to leave our world behind, and Jesus valued the same ordinary things we do—the pleasure of a simple meal shared with friends, the satisfaction of conversation with sensitive companions. Why then is it so hard to remember the common denominator of all human experience—this essential instinct for self-preservation—when we think of him? Jesus would not have spent much time agonizing over his fate if Death were nothing more than a welcome visitor, if he had been willing to accept martyrdom with relaxed indifference.

Perhaps it is the distance of centuries and the mists of piety that keep the real Jesus from us, for assuredly he was troubled by what he saw waiting. Yet in this scene in the Passion drama, the Gospel stories emphasize his unfailing patience and calm politeness to those who are threatening his very existence. The atmosphere of unbearable anxiety and turbulent emotion that surrounded the troubled watcher in the garden has disappeared. And in its place is something more than resignation. It is acceptance.

Here was a rabbi who had sat day after day in the Temple, teaching a message of love and forgiveness, and finally this message was tested by a hostile mob armed with swords and clubs. How did Jesus

The crowds grow . . . and the high priests take notice

react? He reacted in a way that has confused us for centuries. We see patience and mistake it for weakness; we see serenity and then think this means indifference. There is a great distance between the passive resignation of an unwilling victim, and the active acceptance of one who makes a choice from strength and conviction. Jesus may have been the quintessential unarmed civilian, the exact opposite of those who have been corrupted through violence, but he was never timid or shy.

When we confront the serious problems of life, do we respond like Jesus, with an acceptance rooted in our strong faith in a loving Providence? Sometimes we react by drawing our swords, literally or figuratively, lashing out at our enemies with well-chosen words, sharp political manoeuvres or ruthless financial manipulations, determined to rely exclusively on our own strength and ability. So much for our willingness to trust in God's help. At other times, we retreat into a shell of despair, hopeless of ever finding any possible resolution to our difficulties. Once again, we block ourselves off from the greatest Source of power and strength that we could find, convinced that we will fail on the basis of our own inadequacies. How hard it is to accept the gift of grace!

*Lord, I too have trouble understanding the
difference between gentleness and weakness,
strength and aggression. I wish that I could accept
the challenges of my life with perseverance and
dignity, but sometimes I react like the disciple who
pulled out his sword. At other times when I should
be taking action, I retreat into silence and
discouragement. Help me to follow you with
wisdom.*

4

"All of them deserted him and fled"

Mark 14:50

Courage is a virtue rooted in honesty, for the truly brave are those who recognize within themselves the existence of fear and the potential for cowardice. On the other hand, those who are not heroes often disguise their cowardly behaviour with empty threats and idle boasts. When we indulge in the deception of cowardice, the true punishment for failing to proceed with courage lies within our own hearts: however we manage to hide our behaviour from the outside world, we cannot run away from our own memories.

Whatever Jesus felt when he saw his disciples melt away into the night—disappointment, surprise, perhaps even anger—his feelings were soon to be overwhelmed by other realities: the threat of an armed mob bent on violence. This was not the time to reflect on his followers' behaviour! But instantly, as soon as Jesus disappeared from view, those who had not stood by him were left with one appalling thought: "What have we done?" Or better still, "What have we failed to do?"

At some point Peter would slink away to follow Jesus at a safe distance, eventually rejoining James and John and the others, perhaps in a relative's home, or an out-of-the-way tavern, or even in a remote garden or field outside the city. Once they felt safe from the interest of the soldiers and the chief priests, the disciples might reflect on this catastrophe. And then they would talk.

As anyone who has ever made the wrong decision knows only too well, the followers of Jesus could have found plenty of subjects for their unhappy conversations. We can imagine the accusations: "If only I had done this!" and "Why didn't you do that?" We can still hear the questions and answers trailing off into argument or silence, the bitter regrets and recriminations left hanging in the air. In desperation, crazy schemes and impossible solutions might be proposed. We cannot reconstruct any of this scene except in our imagination—and all of us who have experienced similar regrets will find much to imagine—but history does provide us with one undisputed fact. Whatever discussion took place, and

The disciples discuss the capture of Jesus

regardless of the plans that might have been hatched, nothing was ever done. We are certain of this "nothing," for the disciples' disappearance created one great gaping hole of emptiness around Jesus. He was left to stand alone.

One question would be especially painful for the disciples to contemplate during the long hours of waiting for news: "What is going to happen to us?" We can readily understand their inflamed nerves startled by every approaching footstep and every sudden noise. And their fearful speculations: "Are they coming for us next? Where can we go in safety? How can we get hold of some money, some weapons, some supplies?" And being decent people, sooner or later their thoughts would turn to their captured friend and his probable fate. None of this would make for pleasant company during that first Holy Thursday night.

The disciples might have accurately predicted the outcome of Jesus' eventual trial before his enemies; in those hours of waiting, they also had plenty of time to think of all that they might have rejected when they turned their backs and ran away. Some of the older and wiser followers may have been familiar with the corroding effects of guilt, and they could have told the others that it is possible to dwell on the mistakes of the past for days and weeks and even years, consuming the brightness of one's future in bitterness and remorse. None of them could yet imagine the depth of forgiveness that would belong to their experience of the Easter message. None of them could imagine that their story might still have a happy ending.

> *Lord, many of us know all too much about guilt, shame and regret. We may understand something in theory about your forgiveness, but we haven't yet learned to accept this grace in our hearts. Help me to put the past behind as I stretch out my hands to take the gift you freely offer—a chance to start over again in your friendship.*

5

Jesus appears before Caiaphas

Mark 14:53-64

There were many special silences that marked the scenes of Jesus' Passion, but none more intriguing than the ones which interrupted the trial before Caiaphas, the high priest. Jesus remained silent after the false witnesses presented their evidence, prompting the high priest to confront him directly: "Have you no answer?" Finally Caiaphas was forced to put that impossible question into words: "Are you the Messiah?" Only then was Jesus able to respond, "I am."

There is a silence that resonates down through the ages, and underneath can be heard a confusion of unspoken wishes, whispered hints and barely intelligible voices, all of them echoes of the very same words that Caiaphas directed at Jesus. This same silence is present when we struggle to recognize the divine at work in our lives, when we consider the question asked during that painful interview so many centuries ago: "Are you the Messiah?"

The chief priest heard the answer and responded in anger and mounting frustration; he tore his clothes, the traditional way of expressing grief and rage in those days, and accused Jesus of blasphemy. The council all agreed and unanimously condemned their prisoner to death. We too hear the answer, the simple words "I am," and yet there remain questions and doubts. We lose ourselves in the silence that must endure, the emptiness that continues to echo all around and through us. "Are you the Messiah?"

Sometimes we see and feel the existence of God everywhere in our world; we rejoice in this presence, glad to believe in the Creator of bright summer days. It is easy at that moment to walk in the sunshine and work for the coming of the Kingdom. Then another day dawns, and for no really good reason, all the former brightness and peace fades away, nothing remaining but a vague memory lurking inside, shadowy and indistinct. We have to force ourselves to think about this Mystery; even the simplest prayers get stuck in a dry and unwilling throat. The message of Jesus' life has ceased to be real; he has moved out to the periphery of our world, no longer someone who has grabbed hold of us with a tenacity worthy of God himself and to whom we cling with all the perseverance and fortitude of real saints. On those bad days, it is easy to imagine Jesus standing there, head bowed and remaining silent, just as he did in front of Caiaphas. He is not saying anything and the only question we can phrase has already been asked: "Are you really the Messiah?"

Caiaphas wanted certainty; he wanted proof. He may have heard rumours of Jesus' activities with the poor, the sick and the lost; he may have seen him teaching day after day in the Temple. These actions were not enough; it did not seem possible that God's Anointed could really be standing there before him in a linen shift and dusty sandals. Perhaps he imagined a Messiah who belonged up there in the clouds, wearing a belt of flashing light and speaking in a voice like thunder. Or perhaps the Messiah of his dreams would show more interest in the political situation of the day, riding through the desert at the head of a charging army, brandishing a very real sword in his powerful right arm. In both cases, the Jesus who spoke with an ordinary voice, using parables and stories drawn from ordinary life, was bound to be a disappointment.

Caiaphas called on a number of false witnesses during Jesus' trial, witnesses who took a scrap of the truth and twisted it to create some semblance of blasphemy. Caiaphas is long gone, but there are still false witnesses who wander through our thoughts during those dark moments of doubt. We hear whispers that perhaps we are foolishly trying to create a God where there was only a revered teacher or an influential philosopher. We hear suggestions that Jesus' message is little more than a decent code of civilized behaviour, like an ancient etiquette book that still has one or two applications today. If we have any courage, we will recognize that silence must be part of all our encounters with the Word-made-flesh, until the day when we can finally meet face to face.

> Lord, I believe; help my unbelief. When you don't seem to be close at hand, let me remember you standing silently in front of Caiaphas. I need to accept that silence with patience; I will hear it all through my life. When you stand before me in today's world, dressed in the clothes of poverty and need, help me then to recognize you.

6

Peter's denial

Mark 14:66-72

Imagine a large house with many rooms, perhaps a mansion cared for by a small army of servants. There is a courtyard in the centre, a beautiful outdoor space decorated by the pots of flowers that grow so abundantly in the hot Mediterranean sun. Day or night there are always people milling around: some of the servants, of course, plus a few hangers-on as befits the home of an important personage like a high priest: people begging a favour, looking for work, seeking information, delivering messages from other important personages. Inside, in one of the large official rooms, a travesty of a trial is taking place, and Jesus is standing in silence before Caiaphas. Outside in the courtyard open to the sky, Peter settles in to wait with the other bystanders.

At first no one notices this stranger warming his hands in front of the fire, keeping off the chill of the night air and listening with special attention to any rumours that might be circulating. There are a few torches and lanterns throwing out a little light in the gloomy darkness, but the courtyard is a large space, and not too bright. A fellow ought to be safe enough here.

The actors are assembled, ready for this scene of the Passion drama, but when the action starts, it seems more like a witty farce or a light-hearted comic opera: the clever and observant maidservant with the ready wit recognizes Peter! If it were not so unbearably frightening, it would be funny. And with her easy familiarity (after all, she is a servant in an important household) she insists on sharing her observation with the others. Here is something to liven up the night air, some decent gossip for a change, instead of the usual trivialities and speculations that pass for conversation during the tedious hours of waiting. And good sport too: someone new to tease and, by the look of things, very easily riled. He denies it? Of course he does, any fool would, and oh, he squirms uncomfortably. She keeps up the questioning; why stop now just when things are getting interesting? Soon the other bystanders take up the same theme; someone with an ear for accents notices that Peter is from Galilee and remembers that this Jesus, the supposed Messiah, is also a Galilean. How the stranger curses and storms and turns red, pretending not to know the man! Silly fool, as if anyone cares.

And Peter thinking to himself, thinking only of himself, "Where could she possibly have seen me? At one of the vast outdoor assemblies when *he* preached to the crowds? In the marketplace when *he* always seemed to be surrounded by women and children? Out on the road somewhere, on one of the days when *he* healed so many who were suffering? I can understand that she might remember *him*, for he spent most of his time in the last few years living in the public eye. But how could she recognize me? There were always dozens of people around; why would she notice me? What makes me so special?"

The scene that begins like a comedy ends with the tears of a strong and decent man, overcome by his own fear and weakness, remorse and shame. This is the person who will one day face his own death with courage, sustained by his belief in the friend he has just denied; the person who has gone down in history as Saint Peter, in whose honour the most famous church in the world was constructed, and in whose footsteps hundreds of church leaders have followed. It should be a comfort for us to remember Peter, not as he has been commemorated in massive bronze statues and gigantic paintings, but as he sat that night in the cold stone courtyard, head in his hands and tears in his eyes. He will carry the remembrance of this night with him to the end of his days, yet he is still special, even memorable. With his secret dreads and unhappy memories, in need of forgiveness but capable of greatness, he is one of us.

When you were in trouble, Lord, your closest friends pretended not to know you, and yet you never desert us when we need your help. Too often I think I have to stand alone to face whatever problems life has in store for me. Help me to remember that, regardless of my failings, you will never abandon me.

7

Jesus in prison

Mark 15:1

Sometimes there are dark and curious shadows that lie behind the quiet, subtle phrases of the Gospel stories. When we really listen to the beginning of Chapter 15 of Mark's Gospel, we are drawn back in our imaginations to the darkness of the first Holy Thursday night: those hours before Jesus' final trial with Pontius Pilate. Chapter 15, like so many of Mark's stories, begins very simply: "And as soon as it was morning . . . ." This "morning" does not conjure up the cheerful image of a bright new day after a night of refreshing sleep. Rather, this "morning" reminds us of the events of the preceding night, events which we do not fully understand even now. After his interview with Caiaphas the high priest, where did Jesus go for the rest of the night? Was he under guard in some sort of prison? If we reflect on the simple words of Mark's Gospel, we will see a dimension to Jesus' suffering that might surprise us.

Most of us have never been in any sort of prison; whatever we know about that shadowy underworld comes from the more-or-less sanitized picture provided by our mass media. Those who know something about penal systems talk about "deprivation of liberty" when describing the punishment associated with confinement. This is probably because today's institutions are relatively humane places compared to jails in the past. Whatever soul-numbing tortures our overcrowded cells may hold, most inmates do manage to emerge alive, however scarred inside; historians would confirm that, in ancient days, mere survival was considerably more difficult. In any case, prison is a relatively benign term; Jesus probably spent his last night in something that should more properly be called a dungeon.

A small hole in the ground, virtually a pit; an underground cage not even fit for animals; dark, probably damp, if not downright wet; more like a well than a room; either suffocatingly hot or numbingly cold; putrid with the smell of disease and decay. Archaeologists suggest that Jesus would have been dumped in just such a place after Caiaphas had finished with him. And like every other prison, this place was filled with a great emptiness of desolation; the fear of countless other unfortunate captives had soaked right into the filthy walls, and assuredly that was Jesus' companion too. He shared in that

Jesus in prison

loneliness and fear just as he shared in everything else that we know in our human lives.

Many of our thoughts about the Passion of Jesus have traditionally focused on physical suffering; when we first try to concentrate on this story, we need to count the wounds, paint a picture of the cross. With time we learn that suffering comes in many forms: suffering caused by rejection, suffering brought on by memory, suffering heightened by the perception of failure. And in the darkness of that night, wherever he might have been, Jesus' thoughts would have been shot through with suffering. Everything he once believed about his life was now challenged by the darkness of disappointment; the past and the future suddenly took on a sad new meaning. Once he might have looked back with satisfaction on his work, his miracles, his teaching. That understanding of the past had now vanished, and in its place were strange and unsettling emotions—anxiety, uncertainty, dread, confusion.

For a few hours, Jesus was left to recognize his isolation; to wonder about the safety of his mother and his friends; to make sense of his memories of Judas; to regret that his preaching had failed to touch those in command; to imagine all that might happen in the next few days. When we start to think about Jesus' suffering in this way, we put aside the physical dimension of the Passion, and let the mental anguish speak to us instead.

> *Lord, it is frightening to think of the many things*
> *that a human person can endure: a body wasted*
> *by diseases such as cancer and AIDS; a mind*
> *tortured by depression or delusion. I find myself*
> *paralysed by the prospect of such suffering,*
> *haunted by the fear of what might be waiting for*
> *me. Help me to remember that you will be there,*
> *regardless of the places where I may find myself.*

8

Jesus before Pontius Pilate

John 19:1-16, and others

Imagine you were picking the cast for a production of a Passion Play, and think of the sort of actor you would choose for the role of Pontius Pilate. Perhaps you would select someone in middle age with a body that had already started to go soft from too much easy living and not enough hard exercise; someone who looked like a successful politician, not a respected statesman; someone who had cultivated the supercilious smile, the raised eyebrow, the disdainful look. Someone who could turn to Jesus and say "What is Truth?", then walk away in contempt.

Each of the Gospel narratives presents some aspect of Jesus' trial before Pontius Pilate; in our imaginations we combine all the little details to form one composite picture representing Insincerity and Injustice. From Matthew we remember the famous washing of the hands, Pilate's public attempt to absolve himself of any responsibility for Jesus' death.

Mark describes Pilate's desire to satisfy the crowd by condemning Jesus in place of Barabbas, suggesting to us that Pilate was a crafty manipulator who had little interest in justice but great instincts for popular politics. Luke and John show a weak ruler torn between his own verdict and the threats of the crowd. John also contributes the memorable scene in which Pilate is confronted by the reality of Jesus' spiritual kingdom. Jesus reminds his listeners that he came into the world to testify to the truth; Pilate counters this statement with his cynical question, "What is Truth?" Taken all together, the picture that has emerged of Pontius Pilate is not an attractive one.

Pilate's question, however, is notoriously difficult to answer. We can study and examine and struggle and explore, but Truth does not want to be tied down to finite, limited human words. We claim to believe in the Truth of Jesus' teaching, but there is often a vast gulf between the Sunday morning understanding of his message and the weekday applications. Is there one Christian perspective in economic theory, one Christian political philosophy, one Christian ethic that neatly fits all possible earthly situations? If there is, it is hard to put it into words. We may loudly profess one faith in the risen Christ, but we are not as confident when it comes to an interpretation of that event in the context of our day-to-day lives. If it is true that Jesus has come to save all of us, how then should we handle all the contentious issues—social justice, minority rights, environmental respect—that bother most sensitive observers? Some of us line up on the conservative side of the political fence; others are more comfortable with the liberals. Both sides are convinced of the truth of their own positions; both sides have the verbal ammunition to denounce those who disagree with them. It is also possible that real Truth lies somewhere outside the arena of dispute and argument altogether.

The struggle to find Truth is bound to lead us into thorny territory. Unfortunately, once we have learned to manipulate human language, it is all too easy to make this rough road seem smooth. We can learn to converse, debate—even pray!—with grace, style and imagination, regardless of the doubts and anxieties that lurk inside us. We can avoid thinking clearly and deeply about the meaning of Jesus' life for a long time. Honesty and its handmaid, Humility, on the other hand, are uncomfortable and unnerving virtues; it is much easier to hide behind artfully expressed and carefully researched "facts." We don't need to be disturbed by such difficult questions as "What is Truth?" once we have discovered the pleasure that comes from arranging words and phrases, statistics and scientific data into some dazzling, even intimidating, display of knowledge.

If we are honest, however, we come to realize that the search for Truth involves much painful and challenging soul-searching. If we are not a little troubled by what we sometimes see and experience, we are settling instead for some pale imitation, like blandly inoffensive background music that disturbs no one but has little artistic merit either. Unless we are willing to shake up our inner peace and take a few risks with our thoughts and actions, we will eventually find ourselves there with Pontius Pilate: successful, safe and shallow.

Lord, I do not know all the answers; unless I take that fact as my starting point, I will never be able to get close to you. Furthermore, some of what I do know is hard to express and difficult to share with others. You recognize the Truth that lies buried deep within me, even when I am unsure myself. Help me to persevere in my lifelong search for understanding.

9

Barabbas

Mark 15:6-15

Pilate asked his rhetorical question, "What is Truth?", but he hardly expected an answer. The ancient Greek philosophers debated "What is Justice?"; they too never arrived at a totally convincing explanation. Then came the day when Barabbas walked away from certain death, while Jesus was handed over to be crucified. Barabbas doesn't sound like the sort of character who would waste much time debating philosophical niceties; he was "in prison with the rebels who had committed murder during the uprising." But for one brief moment when the prison doors opened and he saw blue sky and open roads, he might have thought to himself, "Truth and Justice don't always win; this time I was lucky."

There is a little of Barabbas in everyone, times when we are saved by a surprising twist of fate from well-deserved failure, ridicule, or exposure. The unexpected windfall that gets us out of trouble with the bank; the freak snowstorm that cancels the examination for which we aren't prepared; the inspection that is postponed long enough for us to clean up the office: we all know about these small—and not so small—graces that protect us from the consequences of our own actions and give us a second chance.

Or sometimes we win because someone else had to lose. Our little misbehaviour is ignored because of a huge public scandal elsewhere; the world overlooks our small failures because someone else's major catastrophe is even more interesting. We walk away free, while others are called upon to explain their mistakes, and we too can say, "This time I was lucky."

If we believe that nothing happens by accident, we might take a moment to wonder about the actions of Providence. Did Barabbas deserve to be spared? No one has ever suggested that he was wrongfully imprisoned and the crowd's actions merely corrected some terrible miscarriage of justice. Any celestial computer that is tallying up our individual vices and virtues doesn't hand out rewards or punishments according to what we deserve *right now*. It is impossible to explain the reason why good doesn't always appear to triumph, and better still, why the wicked (or at least the foolish) are sometimes allowed to walk away free, but we all know that this happens.

Furthermore, the God of second chances lets us experience the blessing of new beginnings on a regular basis, thanks to that surprising gift called Morning. Each and every day of our lives we are given another opportunity to put yesterday and all its mistakes behind, to start over again with a clean slate and revived energy. We can attempt, once again, to get back to our fitness routine; we can try, for the umpteenth time, to keep our temper under control; we can renew, as we have done so often in the past, our determination to live in a way that befits our calling as children of a loving God. And if we fail this time, there will be yet another morning, another tomorrow when we can begin again in hope.

Did Barabbas feel any gratitude for his un-expected reprieve? We will never know. Do we feel gratitude when a fortunate accident gets us out of trouble? Sometimes. Once in a while, we may fall down on our knees—literally—in shock and thanks-giving, when all turns out for the best in spite of our little misadventures; other times, we barely acknowl-edge that Someone has protected us from our own follies. Worst of all are the moments when we laugh and shrug our shoulders in arrogance, as if we have been singled out to live a charmed life, Luck there permanently at our side. Barabbas, in any case, fades out of the picture after his one appearance at this crucial moment in Jesus' story. Our lives continue, morning follows evening, with second and third chances to correct our mistakes, and ever-renewed opportunities to whisper our thanks for blessings received, even when we can't imagine why we deserve them.

> Lord, you have come to my rescue more times
> than I can count and more times than I deserve.
> Or at least, more times than I understand; it is
> not up to me to measure exactly what I deserve.
> In your wisdom you have saved me from myself,
> perhaps so that I may do something for you that I
> am yet unable to imagine. Help me to feel
> gratitude for all these unexpected blessings.

10

Jesus is sent to be scourged

Mark 15:15

Not long ago, an archaeologist working in Old Jerusalem claimed to have found the pillar at which Jesus was scourged. The details of this excavation were reported in the daily newspapers, not exactly the sort of article one wants to read while munching on a bowl of breakfast cereal before beginning the morning's activities. But regardless of the time of day or the state of one's nerves, it would not have been pleasant to study this news item with any great care. For if there is one moment of Jesus' passion that makes many of us distinctly uneasy, it is this: the Scourging at the Pillar.

Something about beatings is especially trouble-some today; many of us are loathe to contemplate anything that might stir up painful memories of childhood punishment or domestic violence. Those of us who live with gentleness are equally ill-prepared to reflect on this brutality, for in our sensitive imaginations we fear what we have never experienced. The experts on Roman crucifixion practice have told us that the preliminary scourging was an ironic cruelty, for the loss of blood would hasten the victim's ultimate death and lessen his sufferings later. The traditional illustrations of this part of the Passion are terrible enough; the historical truth is probably even worse. None of this—our own fears and the historian's research—makes it easy to think, let alone write, about Jesus being scourged.

And yet human beings for thousands of years have inflicted this sort of cruelty on one another. Recently, one of the glossy news magazines carried a photograph of a young boy being beaten with a cane by a soldier in some occupied territory. The boy, perhaps eleven or twelve years old, was lying on the ground, mouth open in a scream that was silent on the magazine page, a scream that echoed in my head for hours later. From what deeply rooted vein of twisted ugliness do we find it in our hearts to treat each other in this way?

While Jesus was being beaten, maybe in the very same room which the archaeologists found, no doubt there were onlookers who followed the proceedings with enjoyment. That sort of sadism still persists today, another frightening thought, for there have always been those among us who derive pleasure from another's pain. In any case, most of us would not have been there watching; we would have fled like all the other disciples. Even from the vantage point of the late twentieth century, it is difficult to keep vigil during this ordeal.

There are so many moments during our lives when we need to ask Jesus' forgiveness for having deserted him, usually because we refuse to recognize that it is really our wounded Lord who suffers when we neglect the sick and the poor of this world. Equally sad are the times when we turn away from divine grace during our own pain. Our faith tells us that Someone is standing there beside us, ready to share in our torments however trivial they might seem to the outside world, and sometimes we refuse to recognize this. Perhaps we prefer to wallow in our own misery for a while, playing the martyr, nursing secret hopes of revenge or even abandoning ourselves to a sort of pleasurable despair. In our arrogance we proclaim that we don't need any help; in our pride, we refuse to admit any weakness; in our laziness, we don't make the effort to remember any words of hope. Such irony: we can't look at Jesus in his suffering and sometimes we can't bear to let him watch with us either.

Lord, I don't usually talk about things like whips or scourgings or lashes, but I know something about suffering. All of us do. Too often when I

*am in pain, I try to be brave and stoical, ignoring
your healing presence, just as I try to avoid
thinking about you during the terrible moments of
your life. Help me to be a faithful witness to your
suffering; teach me to accept your help during
mine.*

11

The crown of thorns

Mark 15:17

An amusing little game: dress the prisoner in an old purple cloak (purple being the official symbol of power in the Empire), then stage a mock coronation using a thorn branch twisted into a crown. A clever little game: a nice way to combine insults and injuries *and* to kill a few hours before the real business of execution can begin. And appropriate too: the perfect treatment of one who was supposed to have mysterious and revolutionary plans for a "Kingdom." When we think about this scene, we may close our eyes to the thorns; it is hard to escape the sound of rough voices taunting Jesus with the local version of that universal proverb, "Let the punishment fit the crime." The laughter is as painful to contemplate as the blood starting to trickle from the wounded forehead.

Twisted, clever, cruel: to take a branch from a living, blooming tree, something that was once green and alive, and turn it into an unusual but efficient instrument of torture. Perhaps the branch came from a hawthorn bush, one of the scrubby little trees that bloom early in the year, just the sort of place where songbirds like to nest in the spring, returning in the autumn to eat the berries; a good tree to have around if you are an industrious farmer interested in keeping bees and making honey. Twisted, clever, cruel: to take a person's innocent ideas and distort them into something vaguely familiar, for, with great irony, the soldiers' taunts contain an undeniable element of truth. Jesus' enemies understood something about the Kingdom he proclaimed, but they made a serious mistake thinking their crown was the emblem of some final defeat.

And what was the measure of Jesus' patience when they dragged out the dirty, maybe even bloody purple cloak? It seems that this game might have been played once or twice before, on other hapless and defeated prisoners who were forced to abandon all hope at the hands of some laughing Roman soldier. With what thoughts of sadness and regret did Jesus watch as his plans for a new Kingdom of peace and forgiveness were unceremoniously dismantled in front of his eyes?

Our reflections about the crown of thorns scratch and dig under the skin, tearing away at the distance of time and space that separates us from Jesus

The mocking of Jesus

and his world, for we are reluctantly reminded of the many ways in which we too have played the same games as those Roman soldiers. We may not turn the ordinary raw material of life into instruments of torture; there are other ways in which we express all the bitterness, anger and envy that lies buried within the shadow of the human soul. The spectacle of human ingenuity can be truly disheartening: twisted, clever, cruel.

So let's not be too hard on those flea-bitten Roman soldiers who were victims themselves, kicked around by fate and their superior officers. We share in their guilt when we twist the truth a little in an effort to justify our own point of view, usually at someone else's expense. We boast of the cleverness with which we defend our own interests; we savour the pleasures of verbal revenge, waiting for the right opportunity to repay some insult, real or imagined. If only we could take a moment, before we speak with cruelty disguised as conversation—the "devastating" brilliance and "razor-sharp wit"—and then we might see ourselves back in time. There is the courtyard of the palace, the soldiers milling around and looking for mischief. We would hear how hollow our laughter sounds to One who knows very well what it is like to be mocked. Forgive us all, Lord, for the times when we were there, plaiting innocent branches from a hawthorn bush into that crown of thorns.

Lord, my tongue is the most dangerous weapon I have; it is all too easy to hurt others through my thoughtless and unkind words. I would never dream of using any real violence, but I should be ashamed of the many times that I have caused pain through my criticism or complaints. Help me to speak with the charity that you came here to teach.

12

Insults by the soldiers

Mark 15:18-20

Humanity has a deep-seated horror of mockery; in fact, "being laughed at" is right up there next to death itself in the unholy litany of Things All People Fear. Think of an experience you have tried hard to forget: the day you made a fool of yourself at a meeting and everyone laughed; the time when the teacher made fun of you in front of the whole class and you started to cry. All of us have something like this buried deep within our hearts; the memory of just such an incident helps us to remain with Jesus during the moments of his Passion when the soldiers added insult to injury and mocked him.

These soldiers bowed down in disdainful reverence to a man who never asked to be treated like a king, who lived a simple life in the company of followers who came from the ordinary working people of his day. Imagine the horror that Jesus felt when he heard the soldiers' words, their implied insult that he was no better than the pompous and self-important figures who revel in all the outward signs of royal power: the formal salutes, fancy titles and ceremonial robes that some of our more petty-minded leaders still demand today. When the soldiers struck his head with a reed, their ludicrous imitation of the sceptre of royalty, we are immediately struck by the contrast between their understanding of this person and our own. We know that Jesus never talked about his Kingdom in words that conjured up visions of crowns, castles and liveried retainers; he rebuked those around him who looked forward to the day when they too might share in his royal reign. He didn't discuss his plans in the exaggerated language that military conquerors and successful politicians love; he couldn't rely on words that resonate with the confident, even boastful, sounds of power. Instead, his mysterious, evocative parables used sensitive, poetic images—the mustard seed, the pearl of great price, the wedding feast—to describe a time and place where justice, not force, would triumph, when truth and love, not luxury and pride, would rule. And now he had to listen in silence to those who distorted his words. What did this mockery feel like to him?

Psychologists say that human behaviour is influenced by the universal hunger for self-esteem. When we let ourselves remember some of the words and phrases that once chipped away at our self-esteem, the bond between Jesus' life and ours is emphasized once again. And aware of our own responses to verbal abuse, we wonder about his reactions and emotions. Did he feel a wellspring of anger bubbling up through his sweat and blood, anger at the ignorant and impudent voices mocking the undeniable truth of his new Kingdom? Was there a faint wisp of doubt that began to seep into his soul, as the effects of hunger, sleeplessness and physical pain started to make themselves felt on his human body? Did he struggle inside against the futility and weakness of his position, raging with all his heart because he could say nothing? We don't know, but remembering our own reactions to humiliation—tears of shame and anger; an unsteady voice and pounding heart—we can share in the sadness of this scene.

Most of the suffering caused by insults and humiliation might not seem very dramatic in a world conditioned to abuse, both mental and physical. We may even feel a little shamefaced at our reactions to mere words, however insulting. Yet humiliation and embarrassment are real enough and never as trivial as we might pretend. We might joke about our social lapses, the silly accidents, the amusing mishaps of daily life, but unkind laughter and mocking words can hurt us more deeply than we would ever wish to admit. Remember the old rhyme from childhood,

"Sticks and stones can break my bones/But names can never hurt me"? Whoever wrote that verse knew very little about the human heart.

> *Lord, I am embarrassed by my thin skin and oversensitive nature; I am not as strong or as patient or as resilient as I would like to be. Criticism, no matter how justified, bothers me; doubts and regrets disturb my serenity. Help me to recognize this human limitation; help me to cope with the insults from the past that still give me pain here in the present.*

13

Carrying the cross

John 19:17

In the long march of evolution, the human race has emerged as a unique species—the only animals to walk upright all the time. The activities of our earliest ancestors influenced the shapes our bodies still retain. Our strong legs originally evolved to carry us far across the plains of prehistoric Africa and Asia in search of food and water; our strong arms and shoulders to carry the fruits of our labours back to the caves and shelters of primitive humanity. We were built to walk and wander. Later on, as civilization progressed, our ancestors still found themselves carrying things: a sack of grain to the mill, a baby or a small animal in a sling, a jar of water from the well, an offering to the Temple. Today our burdens are different again—armloads of library books for students young and old; bags and boxes of groceries for even the smallest family; the satchels, knapsacks and gym bags that one sees everywhere. But regardless of the contents of all these bags or bottles or boxes, we are destined to spend a little of our time carrying things around every day.

Sometimes we feel downhearted as we muse on the burdens of life, for it does seem that Fate frequently hands us a little too much to carry. Oh, not just the heavy briefcase of homework or the awkward basket of laundry. On miserable afternoons after an unpleasant time in the office, we are tired of carrying the load of Work itself, the inexorable need to earn money in order to put bread on the table day after day. On dreary mornings confronted by the headlines and horror stories of the newspaper, it is the burden of history that is so difficult to carry: the depressing age-old chronicle of futility and neglect. Our families and friends can be a source of further strain, as we add the weight of their troubles onto our own already tired shoulders. And even if the calendar manages to squeeze in a week or two of vacation, we know that there will always be tomorrow, bringing more work, more bad news, more demands—more to carry.

In fact, all these major and minor burdens are nothing more than the cross that has been handed to us, and it is maddening to recognize that human nature always tries to escape from it. Escape to a dream world of palm trees and sandy beaches in the "permanent vacation" sort of lifestyle, one without grief, struggle and responsibility. Escape to a fantasy land of glamour and luxury, as if power, status and privilege could somehow protect us from sickness, sorrow or loneliness. Escape from all that we know is imperfect in ourselves in order to bask in the illusion of our own self-righteous saintliness. We are always willing to recount—to ourselves or to any audience that will listen—the litany of troubles that seem to be unique to our lives, convinced that other people's burdens are easier to carry than our own. All the while, we yearn to put down our cross and wander off in search of greener pastures.

And as we indulge in a little self-pity while thinking about the headaches and frustrations of life, we conveniently ignore what we claim to believe: that Someone is down here with us, helping us manage all these exhausting and irritating loads. While we're at it, we forget that he knows even more than we do about carrying burdens. The heavy weight of the cross on the road to Calvary was just the last of these; he also carried the weight of history, the pressure of other people's expectations, the fatigue and anxiety that exists in every human body. Whatever has been handed to us—from the trivial disappointments of everyday living to the most earth-shattering tragedy of a whole lifetime—is little more than a mirror of Jesus' own story. Why do we have such trouble keeping that fact in mind? The answer may be the hardest burden of all for us to carry: the humble acknowledgment of our envious, imperfect and forgetful humanity.

> Lord, you picked up your cross willingly, but
> sometimes I hesitate to accept mine with an equal
> grace. I grow tired of all that I have to carry
> around with me, yet I feel ashamed and resentful
> when reflecting on the example of your perfection.
> Help me to accept that I will always need some
> assistance, no matter what I am carrying.

14

Simon of Cyrene

Mark 15:21

Writers have often wondered about the shadowy figure of Simon of Cyrene. Was he merely a bored and curious visitor to Jerusalem, drawn to the spectacle provided by the parade of Roman soldiers, civil dignitaries and Jewish authorities on the road to Calvary? Was he a pious Jewish pilgrim looking forward to celebrating Passover at the Temple? Mark's Gospel even mentions his sons, "Alexander and Rufus," suggesting to us that Simon and his family were well-known in the early Christian community. Perhaps Simon himself was a clandestine disciple of Jesus, hiding out in the crowd and hoping to catch sight of the Master on this most terrible of days. In any case, Simon was far from home, for Cyrene was a North African seaport with a large Jewish population, a capital city in what is now called Libya, many days' journey from Palestine.

Perhaps Simon started out as nothing more than a travelling merchant or sailor, casually familiar with the many coastal cities in the Mediterranean world. Maybe the Roman overseers picked him out because he was young, healthy and strong, the better to provide some assistance to their victim, now dangerously weakened from beatings that were more severe than the soldiers had intended. Or perhaps they dragged poor Simon out of the crowd because he seemed to be easily intimidated, obviously a newcomer, maybe even servile and a little too eager to please. In any case, regardless of who he was, it is unlikely that he enjoyed taking part in the long walk to the execution grounds.

Imagine the scene: the heavy, ill-finished cross, awkward and rough, hard to carry, full of sharp splinters to scratch at an unprotected arm or shoulder; the condemned man already a little unsteady from loss of blood and general exhaustion; the crowd, armed with new and malicious insults, eager to include the hapless Simon in their taunts; the Roman soldiers and their whips, forcing the procession to move along regardless of the interruptions caused by any stumbles and falls. Poor Simon: he would hardly have chosen to appear in such an unpleasant tableau.

We are sometimes picked out from the crowd just like Simon, and handed some surprising, even unnerving, tasks. There is a mysterious but inescapable hand that seems to guide us through our journeys on this earth, an irresistible force that puts us in one specific place at one specific time. It takes faith to accept that there are no coincidences in life; it is a test of our beliefs to recognize that, in God's eyes, we are always in the right place at the right time. Whether we call these unexpected dispositions of time and space Divine Providence or Luck or Fate, the presence of that invisible hand in human history is impossible to ignore. We may choose to rail against the workings of this mysterious Divinity, resentful of the unexpected summonses and startling developments of life, perhaps even annoyed that our time and talents are called into service for projects beyond our understanding. Or we may graciously accept the accidents that befall us, willing to let ourselves be swept along into something that may prove to be more rewarding than we ever imagined. But whether we react in a positive or negative way, that eternal force will continue to operate, with or without our consent.

What happened to Simon after his little journey on the road with Jesus? Did he return to his previous life untouched by what he had seen, or did he experience some sort of life-changing conversion? When Providence steps into our lives when we least expect it, we are likewise granted an opportunity for change and growth. From the perspective of Calvary, we might find the courage to open ourselves up to the Voice that is calling us, in surprising times and places, with unexpected requests and shocking suggestions. God grant us the wisdom to listen.

> *Lord, a stranger came to your assistance when you least expected it, and you accepted his help with gratitude. Many surprising graces and blessings come my way too, some disguised as accidents and bad luck, but I don't always know how to receive these gifts with humility and faith. I like to think that I know best; help me to recognize that everything you send me—good and bad alike—comes for a reason.*

15

"The place called Golgotha"

Mark 15:22

Italy during Holy Week is a very special place, and not just because of the magnificent liturgies associated with the world-famous churches of Rome, Florence and Venice. Out-of-the-way places far from the usual tourist haunts also celebrate the Easter season with great enthusiasm. Besides the regular services inside the churches and chapels, there are often special outdoor pageants on Good Friday to commemorate the Way of the Cross, or *Via Crucis*. In small towns, this re-enactment of the Passion Story is not exactly like the famous theatrical extravaganzas found under the bright lights of a big city. The costumes have a decidedly homemade flavour: capes and togas are poorly disguised bed sheets; swords and shields little more than foil-covered cardboard. Some of the more sophisticated members of the audience might apologize unnecessarily for the lack of professional flavour, yet the very charm of these pageants lies in their humble and unpretentious origins.

Imagine a warm spring day trailing off into the soft twilight of early evening. Spectators start to line the tiny twisting streets as soon as it is dark, the small family groups waiting, chatting, anticipating. Hundreds of local people will soon be marching by, the first ones representing Old Testament figures—prophets, heroes and villains, complete with scrolls and signs to explain their significance in salvation history. Later on there will be others—apostles and characters from the parables—drawn from the pages of the New Testament. The Good Shepherd appears with a herd of sheep and goats; the children complain that this year the Three Wise Men had no camels. Finally, we see the actors from the Passion story—Judas, Pontius Pilate, the Centurion—and at the end of the procession, a bearded young man dressed as Jesus, shouldering a heavy cross and spurred on by Roman soldiers and their coal-black horses. In the dark, on ancient cobblestone streets lit by torches and moonlight, it is not hard to imagine oneself back in time a few thousand years, on a road very much like the ones that Jesus knew from his ministry in Palestine.

Eventually, the last marchers file by and the audience joins in the procession. Like our predecessors two thousand years before, the pageant finally

Jesus is led through the streets

arrives on a hill at the top of an ancient city; in some Italian towns, the summit may be crowned with the huge stone blocks of a pre-Roman wall, perhaps with the weather-beaten figure of a crouching lion standing guard on one of the cornerstones. And even though we are in the middle of nowhere, watching a performance that lacks the glamour of Hollywood or Broadway, it is very moving to share this witness to Jesus' life and death in the company of ordinary people. Not professional actors or theatre managers or drama students, but ordinary people who feel that it is still important to commemorate these events that happened long ago.

Jesus once arrived at the summit of a hill, a place of blood and violent death: *Golgotha* in Aramaic, *Calvary* its Latinized form, graphically expressed in English as "The Place of the Skull." Ordinary people stood around there too: the same motley collection of spectators, gossips, pickpockets, sensation-seekers, friends and enemies who were part of every crowd he had ever addressed. Some of those who stood there on Golgotha sensed that this person and his suffering were special; others were there only for the spectacle. Some had come to watch the bloodshed and violence for all the wrong reasons; yet because of forces we barely understand, a few of them also went away changed by what they saw.

It is impossible to comprehend faith. Where does it come from? Why does it sometimes desert us? How can we nourish it? Once again, we are confronted with a mystery. Most of us, no matter what our education or upbringing, comprehend only a little of what we are called upon to witness, then or now. Perhaps there are times when we can focus only on the silly little details: the camels (or lack thereof), the costumes, the faces in the crowd. So be it. There is One here with us who understands.

> Lord, your arrival on Calvary marked the end of your road on earth, while for us it stands at the beginning of the mystery of our salvation. You want me to see many things on the journey of my life, people and places that will make me laugh and cry, rejoice and mourn. Help me to appreciate all that is waiting here for me.

16

Jesus is stripped
of his garments

Mark 15:24

His back and legs carried the marks of the scourging he had received a few hours earlier; his shoulders and arms were scratched by the splinters and rough edges of the rugged wooden cross. Besides the welts and cuts and scrapes and abrasions, there were bruises too, left behind by the soldiers in the dungeon and his misadventures on the road. The pain of these wounds, large and small alike, was intensified for one jarring moment when Jesus' clothing was taken from him. At the end of a long and exhausting struggle up the hill of Calvary, more rough hands tore away at his dirty and ragged garments. Not many months before, he had talked with Moses and Elijah on Mount Tabor, his face radiant and his clothing snowy white; now he stood in the company of robbers and outcasts, face streaked with dirt and sweat, his blood-stained clothing in a heap on the ground.

The crucifixion process was intended to involve much humiliation and suffering; even in 33 AD there were simpler and more efficient ways for the state to execute its criminals. All the ugly and horrible details were designed to instil a little wholesome fear into those who regarded all life as cheap, including their own. The respectable citizens in the crowd could righteously watch justice being done, even if justice in this society was rarely tempered with mercy. Those on the fringes of the law would watch more cautiously and perhaps think twice about the possible outcome of their own activities. At least, that has always been the theory behind sadistic public executions. Meanwhile the friends and family of the condemned man would stand by and shudder as they beheld his weakened, blood-smeared body, the last scrap of human dignity stripped away as the criminal was presented, half-naked and pitiable, to the jeering crowd.

Jesus was not the only unfortunate to suffer all the physical pain and psychological trauma of crucifixion, for this was the traditional punishment customarily meted out to bandits and revolutionaries; many before and after him would break into a cold sweat while contemplating the fate waiting for them on a cross. We know this much from sober history books; we can easily imagine the sobs and shrieks that accompanied the suffering of the other victims. When we think about Jesus, however, we often allow ourselves to create an image of superhuman stoicism during all these dreadful moments, because it is too painful to imagine a Saviour who also cries out, or collapses from exhaustion, or shrinks away from the pain.

Is it our overwhelming awe for the self-sacrificing Divinity that makes it difficult for us to dwell on the humanity of Jesus? Perhaps not. It is more likely that we are afraid to see the image of God shattered and reduced to a naked, half-dazed state of such complete abasement. We want—we need!—someone to fulfil our human yearning for perfection, to be the ultimate expression of power and might, lightning bolts flashing, in charge of the four winds and the seven seas, at whose very name the heavens tremble. We don't want to strip away any of the layers we have piled on the Almighty—the many ways in which we have tried to describe Infinity according to our own tastes and talents. And if God has to suffer, at least let it be in stoical silence, with the infinite nobility and patience sanctioned by tradition. But when our mind's eye lingers for a while on Jesus as he stands there on Calvary, we do not see Superman. We see a shivering, semi-delirious victim who knows as much about suffering as any of us.

And this is a sobering thought. If HE can stand there, with all his human dignity and self-possession stripped away, how can we find so much to complain about in our lives? If we are meant to be his followers, perhaps we can start by acknowledging all that insulates us from the truth in his teaching, the layers of pride, anger, laziness and greed that still need to be stripped away before we can truly call ourselves his disciples.

Lord, too often I run away from the truth; sometimes I even try to hide my real self from you. So much in life involves putting on a false face, making a good impression, setting up the right image. Help me to recognize that at least with you I do not have to pretend; you know me as I really am.

The spectacle of the crucifixion

17

"They offered him wine mixed with myrrh"

Mark 15:23

Myrrh is one of those exotic commodities associated with desert caravans and their precious cargoes of valuable spices, rare perfumes and costly silks. Its medicinal properties, as well as its pleasant fragrance, were treasured in ancient times; in a world that relied on herbal medicines and folk remedies, myrrh was evidently used as a sedative. Was it effective? Possibly not, compared to our modern painkillers and narcotics. It was also noticeably bitter. The Roman soldiers offered a mixture of myrrh and wine to Jesus before the Crucifixion was to begin, and no doubt thought their gesture a humane one. For some reason, Jesus refused this drink.

It is a universal human instinct to avoid pain and to prolong our existence in this life for as long as we can manage, by whatever natural or artificial means are available. Every society known to history has looked for ways to deal with the ailments that plague the human body. Toothache, arthritis, childhood maladies, heart disease—the human animal is prey to a host of illnesses, and we have been highly ingenious in alleviating the pain and discomfort that accompany all the stages of life. Jesus, too, was always interested in helping people cope with pain; witness his many healing miracles: curing the paralytic, the blind man, the ten lepers. He certainly did not forget that humanity is a unique blend of body and soul; his mission offered hope for all of us who are beset by illness, mental, physical or spiritual.

Yet when his own time of physical suffering came, Jesus refused the goblet of wine mixed with myrrh. Why? He may have rejected the unfamiliar cup handed to him by a stranger on Calvary merely because he was a little dazed and confused from loss of blood, his actions no longer guided by reason. On the other hand, he may have consciously decided that he preferred to retain some control of his mind for as long as he could, regardless of the pain that would shortly and inevitably be tearing at his body.

Preserving our mental stability can be just as difficult as maintaining the physical well-being of our bodies. Most of us worry a little about losing control through senility or Alzheimer's disease; we watch apprehensively as our older relatives endure a living hell if their minds no longer function. We applaud sensitive documentaries on the sufferings of the mentally ill; we give awards to actors who are able to communicate something of the shadowy world of madness to those of us who are supposedly normal. And deep inside, we wonder if someday we too might lose the ability to distinguish illusion from reality, drifting slowly into some nightmare from which we will never awaken. If I can no longer recognize myself, who will I be?

I could ponder the mystery of self-consciousness forever. If I had to strip everything away from myself: my appearance, my health, my intelligence, my memory—would there be anything remotely resembling "me" left? Something in my faith rather tenuously answers "Yes." Even if I were no longer able to do or think or act or hear or see, there will still be something left; something that might not be terribly interesting to a world that idolizes action, improvement and success, but something valuable nevertheless. Call it my soul or my spirit or whatever new word comes along to convey the intangible and the unmeasurable. Perhaps Jesus also feared that his ability to think and reason and pray and recognize would be taken from him in his last few hours. As I let myself reflect on this, I may find the courage to put myself more fully into his hands, even as I wonder about just who I am.

Lord, many of us wander in a wilderness of mental turmoil; maybe we even contribute to our own confusion through the abuse of drugs and alcohol. The temptation to run away from the pain of reality can be irresistible; we are always looking for something that will offer an easy solution to our problems. Help me to understand what you mean by reality, even when it involves suffering and sacrifice.

18

"And they crucified him"

Mark 15:24

Someone once wrote a sensitive description of suffering and serious illness, with perceptive reflections on the last stages of bodily deterioration. The dying woman in the story explained to her daughter that she kept hold of her sanity in spite of everything she endured because she "listened to her pain." I read about this woman with sadness; nevertheless I was curious about her experience. What did she hear in her body during the dark, sleepless hours of the night? Does pain sound like noise or music? Maybe she was merely hallucinating or indulging in a fanciful dream. This image of the sound of pain comes back to me whenever I think about those moments of the crucifixion that are most difficult to contemplate. And I wonder about the sounds that Jesus heard inside his suffering.

While the last few hours of that dreadful afternoon slowly passed, a multitude of other unhappy events were taking place elsewhere around the world. And other people also listened in pain and fear: to the shattering of bone against metal in the violence of war; to the roar of a storm tossing a fragile boat against the reefs of an uncharted sea; to the hollow emptiness that follows when a sick child's laboured breathing finally turns to deadly silence. Not everyone who suffered on that day was present at The Place of the Skull to hear the hammering of nails into the wood of the cross; yet whatever Jesus experienced in his own pain contained within it some resonance of all the other tears being shed everywhere on this earth.

But while many people heard the sound of pain within their hearts on that first Good Friday, in other places humanity listened to the wonder of God's creation with satisfaction and delight. Newborn babies greeted the day for the first time with cries that filled their mothers' ears with gladness. Children played with balls and tops and wooden toys, laughing with noisy exuberance at the fun and games of childhood. Somewhere an old man whistled as he walked through his garden; a troupe of musicians practised on their flutes and harps; a young bride murmured a few special words in her beloved's ear. The work of life continued as always: a cook listened to the hissing of oil heating up over the fire; a scribe heard his pen scratching across the parchment. All the while, the business of crucifixion continued on Calvary, with its appalling sounds of pain and suffering, and the plan of human salvation continued to unfold. We may recognize the beginning of this process when the angels rejoiced at Jesus' birth, the cold night air resounding to a *Gloria* that reached to the highest heavens. But as the executioner walked up to Jesus, hammer and nails in his hands, my understanding tells me that celestial music once again filled the air with the very same Good News—the news of self-sacrificing love and universal redemption.

Nevertheless, it is hard to feel like singing during this scene; the crucifixion has been traditionally associated with only the most sombre and solemn of sounds. Yet in God's great unbounded present, everything that is touched by divine love is contained in one infinite circle moving through time and space, embracing all history, all thought, all goodness within itself; forming one vast immeasurable never-ending song of praise that has its home wherever God is. The loving and industrious sounds of life and the sobs and groans of tragic suffering belong together. Together they resonate and endure, not fully accepted in human understanding, but taking shape and blossoming in the mind of God.

And if the Light of divine love has come down to earth—and in Jesus we recognize this presence in the most tangible and concrete way—the music of

God's understanding must be here too. It is a hymn that never stops, even if the ugliness of human folly seems to be drowning out its finest voice forever.

> Lord, there are moments when I hear only the indistinct whisperings of my uncertain heart; when I am confused by the mixture of joy and sorrow that belongs to your life. Your message is more than a soothing lullaby or a tranquil pastoral rhapsody; there are moments when you want me to listen—really listen—to discord, strife and noise. Help me to remember that you are with me in all the sounds of life.

19

"Jesus of Nazareth,
King of the Jews"

John 19:19-22

Imagine a map of the Roman Empire, like an illustration from a high school history book, and then think about the tentacles of Roman power and administrative efficiency that reached out to embrace all the known world. Imagine the Roman legal and military experts, followed by farmers and families, who eventually spread across the whole Mediterranean and beyond, bringing their unique brand of civilization to far-flung outposts stretching from Britain to India.

Often while thinking about the details of Jesus' life and death, we find ourselves reminded of Rome and some of its history and traditions. If our understanding of this history has been shaped by Hollywood and Cecil B. DeMille, we may think that civilization in the ancient world was nothing but an endless orgy of dancing girls, insane emperors and handsome gladiators. The inscription on the cross reminds us of another aspect of Roman life.

In John's Gospel, we read that Pilate's judgement of Jesus was "written in Hebrew (that is, Aramaic), Latin and Greek." Greek was the common language of the Eastern Mediterranean; Latin was used by officials and those who looked to Head Office in Rome for instruction and inspiration; Aramaic was the local Semitic tongue, the language that Jesus and his followers spoke. Like many of us today, the residents of the cities under Roman rule knew what it was to live in a multiracial, multicultural society. In other scenes in the New Testament, we are reminded of the dozens of different peoples who were exposed to Jesus' message. Students marvel at the extent of the Roman territories during history class; they may be equally beguiled by all those exotic races living in Jerusalem, the people who were to hear the Good News about this young prophet and his life and work—the Medes and Parthians and Elamites, the inhabitants of all those lands of the Near East, with names echoing the mysterious, romantic past: Mesopotamia, Cappadocia, Phrygia, Pamphylia. In spite of his origins in an insignificant Galilean village, Jesus soon found himself addressing a society that included faces, traditions and customs that were markedly different from his own.

All this ethnic diversity and linguistic variety in first-century Palestine should seem very familiar to us; in the city where I live, the signs in store windows are often written in two, three or even four languages. Unfortunately, the diversity and variety that some of us find so interesting today is often surrounded by resentment, ignorance and unmistakable antagonism. That inscription on Calvary, with its three languages side by side, might indicate a harmony that our society would surely envy.

But Pilate's trilingual sign, "Jesus of Nazareth, King of the Jews," stirred up controversy nevertheless, and no leader back then was a stranger to controversy. We know that the political situation in Palestine, indeed throughout the whole empire, was far from peaceful. Zealots, revolutionaries, factions, plots, rebels, traitors: in spite of the vaunted Roman peace, the *pax Romana*, the world endured the same political chaos that distresses so many of us today. And then there were the religious sects! Jesus and his friends knew what it was to live in a subject country ruled by unfriendly and suspicious overlords; they were surrounded by an on-going struggle for liberation, self-rule and respect. People argued and debated, bickering with each other over race, religion and political affiliation, and no one ever won.

What about Pilate's inscription, the source of the chief priests' displeasure? Some of us who admire

Pilate's multilingual diplomacy also recognize that his choice of words was still not quite accurate. With time and reflection, we have come to understand something about the Kingdom that Jesus preached: a place which has no boundaries of time or space and does not need to be defended by soldiers and treaties, a place with a truly revolutionary understanding of law and authority and obligation. Only in this Kingdom will the inadequacies of all human institutions ever be put right. We have come to understand a little of the reason that Jesus taught us to pray, "Thy Kingdom come."

> *Lord, it is sometimes difficult for me to understand and value the many other races and cultures that now make up my society; it is all too easy to be frightened by change, to find comfort only in familiar faces and customs. Help me to regard newcomers as special, not merely different; help me to feel the same respect for others as I pray that you feel for me.*

20

The soldiers divided up
his clothing

John 19:23-25

Every occupation has its own little rewards and traditional privileges. The family of the baker expects to serve only the freshest bread for dinner; the daughter of a florist hopes to carry the finest bouquet at her wedding. And the soldiers who attended a crucifixion two thousand years ago were allowed to share the condemned man's clothing. Not much of a benefit in our eyes: we have become far too fastidious and accustomed to cleanliness and privacy to think that someone else's torn and blood-stained garments would be worth the trouble of carting home. Anyone who has seen real poverty at close hand knows that, in many other societies, nothing as valuable as cloth would ever be wasted, regardless of how dirty and worn it might be.

And Jesus' garments? A cotton or linen shift, specially hand-woven in one piece, perhaps by one of his many women followers, and therefore a generous length of fabric with many possible uses. Then some outer garment or cloak comprising more large quantities of cloth, for a cloak was an all-purpose garment that could swiftly turn into a blanket or pillow at night, even if stained and threadbare. A head-dress, necessary in the harsh semi-arid climate, shielding its wearer from the fierce heat of the day and the biting wind in a sandstorm and, in a society without umbrellas and raincoats, offering some small protection from the infrequent but drenching rains. A belt made of leather for sturdiness and strength, well-worn but soft and supple with age, also useful for carrying bundles and harnessing stray animals if there is no rope handy. And shoes or sandals, again hand-made as everything would be in the days before factories and mass production, well-used during the years of walking the dusty roads of Palestine. It is this collection of garments that is so valuable to the soldiers; simple clothes with no exotic colours derived from rare, imported dyes; no luxurious silks or brocades; nothing terribly new or fashionable. Plain, serviceable and ordinary.

And somebody wanted them, regardless of their condition or previous ownership. The first readers of the Gospels could readily believe that this pathetic bundle of clothes would be of interest to soldiers. And remember, soldiers were official state employees, not

"And they drew lots for his clothes . . ."

beggars, lepers or street urchins. The soldiers' interest is hard for us to grasp today, when everyone, except the utterly destitute, possesses drawers and cupboards and closets full of clothes—all those shirts, jackets, sweaters and jeans that are necessary here in the twentieth century.

And standing somewhere in the background of this scene is a woman who will be glad to receive that small armload of dirty used clothing; who won't mind in the least having to wash out someone else's sweat and blood to make a piece of fabric useable again; whose back is sometimes sore from bending at the side of a river or by a public fountain, patiently scrubbing out stains and wringing out heavy garments, and whose hands are rough and worn at an early age from too much cold water and hard work. In our technologically advanced society, we can turn on a washing machine and be free of this long and boring drudgery, yet we complain about the inconvenience of housework. Meanwhile, millions and millions of less privileged souls are still, even today, standing there beside fountains and rivers, pounding clothes on rocks and scrubbing them against washboards.

Later on, once Jesus' clothes were a little cleaner, perhaps that same resourceful woman might turn her new-found piece of fabric into something useful for her family: skilfully disguising torn edges or frayed ends, cutting the long length of linen into smaller items for a child, until finally there might be nothing left but a few scraps, still good for rags and bandages. In the abundance of our society, we are free from the necessity of such careful and painstaking labour; but the words of the Gospel stories always take us back to those places where a bundle of old clothes still has value. It is to those in humble surroundings, in sharecroppers' cabins, refugee camps, or charity wards, that Jesus' message still leads us today.

> Lord, I am rarely conscious of the luxuries and privileges of my life in today's society; instead I find a thousand reasons to complain about the interruptions and demands of my everyday existence. Help me to understand the difficulties and obligations that other people face in their day-to-day struggle to live; help me to recognize the many reasons I have to feel gratitude.

21

The two bandits

Mark 15:27

And there were two bandits hanging from their crosses, one on either side of him, their backs and legs also raw from scourging, drenched with some of the same sweat and fear as Jesus, wishing death would come quickly to release them from the misery of aching limbs and painful breathing, cursing inwardly or outwardly the cruel world and personal stupidity that had brought them to Calvary. Standing somewhere in the crowd of spectators might have been a few of their friends and relatives, remembering with regret the wild and wayward boys whose childhood mischief and ungovernable tempers had finally brought them, after a lifetime of petty crime and trouble with the law, to this frightful place.

Someone else might have looked up at the two and thought the world well rid of these sewer rats who preyed on the innocent and the weak, that the state was entirely justified in hammering together those rough wooden crosses to cleanse society of these wicked criminals. Trespassing into the forbidden territory occupied by someone else's goods is a challenge to the whole fabric of civilization, or so we think. And like most societies before and since, the Roman world was quick to punish those who had little respect for the wealth of others.

There have always been those who live by helping themselves to the fruits of another's labour. Scholarly journals soberly describe yesterday's underworld populated by pickpockets and highway robbers. Our contemporary news media report on today's sensational variations: computer fraud, stock market manipulation, pyramid schemes. From old-time legends of swashbuckling pirates on the high seas to the modern sagas of robber barons and industrial espionage, the history of the world is full of bandits of one stripe or another. Some are like the desperate drug addicts waving switchblades and guns in the faces of terrified old ladies on inner-city sidewalks; others are suavely dressed in silk suits, carrying hand-tooled leather briefcases and gold-tipped fountain pens through board rooms, law courts and government offices.

What is at the root of this universal propensity for crime? Is it laziness? Yet many crooks work with great devotion and discipline—almost like those of us in legitimate occupations—spending hours and weeks and years planning and organizing large and small scale operations of bewildering complexity. Is it the excitement of the chase that inspires illicit behaviour? Certainly the company of ruthless drug lords and criminal masterminds might seem to be more potentially stimulating than the conversation of those who spend half their lives on assembly lines or in boring offices, for a while at least. Yet much of the work of crime is tedious in the extreme, involving hours of waiting and watching and study and patience. What about the danger—the risk of prison, torture, death, disgrace? We know that pickpockets and other petty thieves used to do especially good business at public hangings in the old days, not at all inhibited by the presence on the gallows of others just like themselves; so much for the deterrence of swift and terrible punishment! And environment: slums and ghettos contribute their share to the vast underworld of crime, but so do private schools and country clubs.

Here is one of the great mysteries of human life: the universal presence of dishonesty. It is easy to deplore the full-time criminals: the housebreakers and bank robbers and muggers who make life in the city so uncomfortable today. Unfortunately the same tendency to larceny exists nearly everywhere, but we rarely comment when respectable citizens cheat a little on their income taxes, indulge in some creative bookkeeping on their expense accounts, or quarrel with their relatives over the family inheritance. Almost as pervasive as the instinct for self-preservation is our ability to steal from one another.

> Lord, you are in our midst, silent and suffering, and on every side you are surrounded by bandits, for within all of us is the potential for greed and dishonesty. There are times when I cling to my own possessions and look enviously at the wealth of others, as if you had never come here to teach me a lesson of justice and generosity. Help me to cultivate honesty while learning to be more detached from the goods of this world.

22

"Those who passed by mocked him"

Mark 15:29

The victims of crucifixion rarely died quickly from their wounds, lingering instead for hours, sometimes even days, and during this time they often entered into conversations with those who came to watch. From their painful vantage point above the ground, they could argue or pray or lament or implore, or they could suffer in sullen silence. Regardless of the various ways they might react to the comings-and-goings around them, there is one thing that all these crucified souls shared in common: none of them faced death alone. Their sufferings were part of the public spectacle of the day.

Our meditations so often focus on all that Jesus might have seen and thought while looking down at our world reflected in the mirror of the cross. But what did the crowd think while looking up at him? Some of those who gathered there had nothing better to do on a Friday morning than to walk along the Calvary road, morbidly curious about the ravings of the latest victim. Some of those passing by had once heard Jesus preach; perhaps they had listened to his message with a certain scepticism. What did all those high-sounding words about justice and kingdoms and mercy have to do with their miserable lives of frustration anyway? Over the years, they had heard enough plain and fancy speeches from other wandering prophets and wonder workers, yet their prospects remained ever the same. And if they had seen a miracle or two performed by this Galilean preacher, it would soon be shrugged off as bogus trickery, a cleverly staged hoax, little better than the entertainment put on by the travelling jugglers and acrobats who performed for small coins in the dust around the public fountains. The past and the present added up to nothing more than disappointment, a commodity well understood after centuries of waiting for a deliverance that never came. No wonder their laughter was edged with bitterness and cynicism.

There were a few sympathetic believers along with the sceptics who surveyed the three crosses, those who had listened and struggled honestly to understand the parables and lessons. Now all their unformed hopes and silent prayers remained hidden and unanswered. However much they once dared to think that here at last might be the true saviour, that dream was over. Wasn't it? And as we often do when we experience a little disappointment, all of them, sceptic and believer alike, took that bitter lesson and rejected it with sarcasm and mockery.

We do the same thing, when the God of our imagination fails to perform according to our expectations. How many times have we lashed out in anger and disbelief when our precious arrangements for life, love and happiness are turned aside by a Providence whom we profess to honour, not to mention obey? We want to write our own scripts, aided and abetted by a powerful and indulgent God who is sitting "up there," just waiting to move a few mountains and work a few miracles to enhance the drama of our dreams. When we find that other plans have been made for us and no one seems to be answering our prayers, we turn our faces away and respond in disappointment and bitterness, just like those who once before walked by the cross on Calvary.

Meanwhile, Jesus still stays there, the cross silhouetted against the sky; the reality of his life, his suffering and death, have not changed. If our faith has taken root only in the hunger for better days and happier nights, it too will wither in the chilling shade of that dark and blood-stained wood. We can walk by, avoiding the eyes of one who is saying something that we don't want to hear; we can turn away from his face in order to follow another road, a road we are

111

entitled to choose. And still he stays there on the cross.

> *Lord, I wish I could keep from interrupting you when you are speaking to me, but my own thoughts and words always seem more important. I have yet to accept all the surprises you keep sending my way. Help me to listen to your message, instead of endlessly trying to twist your words into something less threatening, less exciting, less challenging than you really mean.*

23

The chief priests and the scribes

Mark 15:31

Their houses were larger and more comfortable than those of the common people, with space set aside for manuscripts and scrolls, important correspondence and official business. There were far more lamps, and better quality ones too, for in these households reading and writing were necessities, not luxuries. Their wives wore clothes of fine linen and soft wool; they treasured a few pieces of jewellery—a gold chain, a brooch to fasten a cloak, some precious stones set in a bracelet or ring. The hands of these women were still soft and smooth, thanks to the servants who took care of the rough and demeaning housework; the wife of the chief priest did not carry water from the public wells or pound grain in a mortar.

Their children were carefully educated, in anticipation of the day when the boys, grown into men, would follow in their fathers' and grandfathers' footsteps in the service of their religion. Good marriages were arranged for the girls, linking prominent families of the community together so that other generations could continue their comfortable, carefully ordered lives. All in all, the prospects of the leaders of this society were radically different from the expectations of the fishermen, farmers and servants who eked out a simple, precarious existence and made up the bulk of the population—those ordinary men and women who were the principal members of Jesus' flock.

The establishment always reacts defensively when its privileges and powers are threatened by change and reform. Who would voluntarily choose to give up pleasant surroundings and the satisfaction of command? And on what grounds? Perhaps the rules and regulations of the old religion were many and strict—it is said that there were 613 commandments outlined in the sacred books—but these were spelled out in the most careful manner, and, after centuries of commentary and debate, the path to virtue was plain for all to see. Then this Son of a carpenter came out of nowhere with his preposterous claims and *new* commandments.

His good-for-nothing cousin, the one they called the Baptist, began his ministry by calling for repentance. Of what was there to repent in their lives? Did they not keep all those laws right to the letter, avoiding every instance of uncleanness, offering the proper sacrifices as commanded in the Torah, saying their prayers with all possible devotion and dignity? They were not like the unwashed common sinners, the men who barely understood the simplest commandment, let alone the complicated code of conduct that the Law prescribed, or the women who were frivolous, impudent, and God knows what else!

Everyone knew that this Jesus actually consorted with public sinners, tax collectors, women of uncertain reputation, inviting them into his home and eating with them. He was as bad as they were with his so-called miracles and signs, the sort of thing that would appeal to the gullible, uneducated masses. Not only was his behaviour outrageous, but his policies were unworkable. How could one turn the other cheek to insults? Why should I love my neighbour, and who is my neighbour anyway? What was this living water that the people babbled about after one of his sermons? A well-run society can hardly afford to look with tolerance upon such disturbers of the fragile and carefully contrived peace. And now look how all this talk of a new Kingdom has ended!

As the chief priests and scribes walked by the cross on Calvary, we can readily imagine some such indignant thoughts passing through their minds.

Looking upon Jesus hanging there, it would seem to them that their side had won. The past could continue to dictate the way of the present, and the future would unfold as they had always known and expected. The mad talk of a Messiah, a new David, a Son of God would fade away soon enough, as it always did whenever one of these false prophets appeared like a plague on the landscape, and life would return to normal. Normal, safe, secure and unchanging.

> *Lord, I don't like change either. I don't blame the people of your day who refused to believe in your new Kingdom. Behind the gentleness of your words there is something frightening and challenging, calling us to renew ourselves in the most radical way. It was hard then; it is still hard now. Help me.*

24

"He saved others; he cannot save himself"

Mark 15:31b

He saved others, and we know some of them by name: Lazarus, Jairus's daughter, Bartimaeus. We know a few of the ailments that plagued them: leprosy, paralysis, blindness. Some who approached him were of high social standing, like the centurion and the leader in the synagogue; others were the lowliest of the lowly, like the blind beggar or the man possessed by an unclean spirit. They came in such numbers that sometimes Jesus had to escape to the countryside for a few hours' rest; they followed him on the street and furtively tried to touch his clothes, believing that even such a silent encounter would prove effective. One memorable time, they boldly removed the clay tiles from the roof so that a paralytic could be let down into the house, so desperate was someone for help. The pages of the Gospels are full of men and women looking for comfort, hope and relief, and some of those who searched went away satisfied.

Jesus saved many people from debilitating illness and pain; a few he saved from death itself. But there were countless others just as worthy of his attention, and in the finite number of days and hours available to him during his public ministry, Jesus met only a fraction of the sick and wounded of this world. He never attempted to heal every leper in Palestine. Furthermore, his miraculous cures did not last forever; those who once experienced his healing presence did not become immune thereafter to future sickness and death. All of them—Peter's mother-in-law; the woman with the haemorrhage; the son of the Widow of Nain—would eventually succumb to some other illness just like the rest of humanity. Eventually and inevitably they all had to taste death itself, the final human experience, exactly as Jesus himself was to do.

The chief priests and the scribes taunted Jesus with his past history of miracle working, ascribing his presence there on the cross to his inability to perform any further wondrous feats. There have been critical observers ever since who have doubted the truth of the various cures and wonderful episodes recounted by the supposedly credulous evangelists. The modern world doesn't like the miraculous or the unscientific. Those of us who try to read the Gospels with an

Jesus healing

openness of mind and heart see the cross on Calvary, not as proof of Jesus' failure, but as one more example of his solidarity with humanity in all that is most normal and natural. We may joke that we "can't escape from death and taxes." Taxation is far from universal, but death assuredly is.

Over and over again we see the threads of universal human experience woven through the details of Jesus' life. He ate and drank like all of us, walked on ordinary roads, stopped to talk to children, asked for a drink of water when he was thirsty, fell asleep when he was tired, mourned the loss of his friends and relatives. He experienced anger and sadness, felt temptation and loneliness; he knew pain, frustration and fear. His parables are remarkable for the wealth of familiar details in which he chose to present his message. What could be more totally human than the portraits he sketched out for his listeners—of a widow sweeping the floor, a farmer sowing in a field, a man inviting guests to a party, a woman mixing yeast and flour together? Image after image reinforce our conviction that Jesus came to save human beings, not angels or sublime spirits who never stumble or fall on their life's journey. He came to speak to us, people who know what it is to suffer and who wish we could be saved from pain and even death itself.

Those who mocked him as he suffered there on the cross would also experience the limitations placed on all earthly existence, for one day they too would find themselves facing death. They would derive little comfort in their last hours from what they had once seen on Calvary; they would have forgotten long before the satisfaction they may have derived from their sarcastic remarks directed at a dying man. "He saved others; he cannot save himself." The significance of his apparent failure to "save himself" would be lost for them.

Lord, you did not save yourself from sorrow and death, yet you never fail to be with those of us who are suffering. You stand here at our bedsides and watch with us when we are frightened and in pain. Help me to overcome my frustration and discouragement in the face of illness, and instead let me recognize the comfort you always bring to anyone who approaches you with faith.

25

"Father, forgive them; for they know not what they do"

Luke 23:34

The Prodigal Son came home and his first act was to beg his long-suffering father's forgiveness, humbly, directly and honestly: "Father, I have sinned." The Tax Collector stood far off in the Temple, head bowed in prayer, recognizing himself to be a sinner: "God, be merciful to me." Peter knelt at Jesus' feet after the great catch of fish, acknowledging his unworthiness: "Depart from me, Lord, for I am a sinful man." There are examples of mercy and pardon on page after page of the Gospels; even the words of the Lord's Prayer remind us to pray for forgiveness. The first of the traditional "Seven Last Words of Christ"[1] begins with the plea, "Father, forgive them";

---

[1] The "last words" are really phrases which occur in the four Gospel accounts of the Passion; there has long been a traditional reverence for them. They often serve as the focus for Lenten meditations and Good Friday devotions, and have been set to music by Haydn and other composers.

forgiveness, then, should be perfectly understandable to us. The problem comes in the second half of this famous verse—"for they know not what they do."

Do we know what we are doing? Sometimes, rarely, often, never? One of the great rallying cries of western civilization has been the insistence on individual responsibility, the fetish we have made of self-reliance, the emphasis that moral teaching has placed on choice and the primacy of the will. There we stand, clutching Freedom and Understanding to our collective breast, ready to proclaim ourselves responsible, unfettered and independent; yet over and over again, we find ourselves falling back on the refrain, "Forgive me." As St. Paul[1] so rightly observed, we do not live as we claim to believe; we choose what we profess to despise. Why?

The existence of sinfulness in the world is hardly ever in dispute. Its origin is harder to explain. Original sin, our fallen nature, temptation and the devil: we try to account for our weaknesses and failings through various words and phrases taken from the pages of some catechism, but we never solve the problem of the existence of evil. Psychologists and those who study human behaviour use another whole lexicon of terms to describe the motivation and rationale behind human actions. But even if

---

[1]   Romans 7:15. In this Epistle Paul deals with themes of salvation, sin, reconciliation, forgiveness.

scientists, doctors or ministers of religion are able to explain our foolish and wicked behaviour, nothing has ever been able to eradicate human failing forever. We can only return to a realization of our fallen state, sometimes with sorrow, but often in anger and resentment, feeling the need of forgiveness and perhaps hating our church and our God for eternally reminding us of the universal human condition: weak, wounded and wrong.

Jesus did not write a theology textbook on sin; he left that thankless job to his followers, some of whom have taken up the challenge with lamentable zeal. We have created detailed categories of sin; we have drawn up elaborate plans for the punishment of sin; we have taught ourselves to fear sin in all its many and glittering forms. Rarely do we admit to ourselves that we are prevented by something built into our very natures from ever understanding, let alone conquering, all human weakness. We used to heap coals of punishment on wrongdoers, either through our highly coloured threats of the hell to come, or by the construction of very real bonfires here on earth. The world's gift of forgiveness has always been tied to an infinity of conditions for repentance and restitution, penance and sorrow. Yet Jesus seems to promise a forgiveness that is rather more freely offered, something unconditional, even incomprehensible, a forgiveness that is tendered before we even understand that we need it.

Perhaps some day we will be able to gather together in a spirit of reconciliation based on true humility and not false pride. We will admit that we understand pathetically little about the human heart; we will put aside the stubborn arrogance that insists on a repentance that seems to derive more from legalism and revenge than from love and compassion. We will let ourselves encounter the generosity of God in a recognition of our own limitations, happy to admit this truth: even when we do not know what we are doing, Jesus wants to offer us his forgiveness.

Lord, if I learn one thing from your suffering, let it be humility. Not some false and grovelling abasement that wants to feed on its own unworthiness, but a trusting hope in the forgiveness that you promised, even in your last moments. Help me to accept what you know me to be, even as I live in this world of weakness and limitations.

26

"Today you will be with me in Paradise"

Luke 23:43

Over the centuries, there has been much specu-
lation on the nature of the Paradise for which we all
yearn; its components seem to vary according to our
individual tastes and dreams. Gustav Mahler
describes a playful Paradise in his Fourth Symphony,
with cakes and games and celestial music; there is a
forthright simplicity to this world as seen through the
eyes of a child, making it especially attractive to
adults who yearn to recapture their own lost
innocence. Dante's *Paradiso* is fittingly austere and
even difficult to comprehend, a contrast to the
entertaining human interest of the *Inferno*. Thousands of jokes and popular stories draw their inspiration from a heaven filled with harps, clouds and
pearly gates, all watched over by a bearded St. Peter
and various wisecracking angels and saints. Jesus
offers no blueprint for eternal happiness in his

127

promise of Paradise; the biblical understanding of the reward of heaven is always vague and undefined. Instead, it is the immediate reality of this Paradise, something that is promised "today," that should strike us so forcefully.

"Living for today" usually conjures up the idea of some selfish hedonist who fails to work hard, invest in a retirement plan and keep house with the discipline and order that respectable society demands. Yet the alternative—"living for tomorrow"—is equally unappealing as practised by those who scrimp and save joylessly, enduring, never enjoying, this present moment, waiting to begin real life at some ever-receding future date. How often do we observe others (or perhaps ourselves) busily chasing a distant goal—of financial security or career achievement—that will finally provide that long-awaited happiness? For those who place all their hopes on tomorrow, the present is merely a stepping-stone to the future, the past so much dead wood, discarded and best forgotten.

And the minutes and days and weeks pass by, adding themselves up into the sum of our years, and many of us are still waiting for something to begin. A restless and nervous energy drives us mercilessly forward, onward, maybe upward, looking for more, striving to be better, hoping to achieve the peace and serenity that has eluded us here on earth, but which is bound to be waiting for us tomorrow in Paradise.

Jesus' words from the cross stand out like some gigantic stop sign posted across the twisted path of those whose anxious searching never ends. He bids us stop to look around at the place where we find ourselves today, to recognize the entrance to his Kingdom right there. In our imperfect world, in spite of sickness, poverty and crime, he asks us to experience his presence now. In our daily pleasures and frustrations, the satisfying family dinner or the annoying rush hour traffic, he invites us to recognize the work of his Father's creation. He wants us to begin living with him wherever we find ourselves, right there in the fabric of an ordinary day. Our meals, our work, our anxieties, our prayers: all the trivial and far from otherworldly business of life can become the ground for experiencing his promise of Paradise. He invites us to begin a new life with him today, not when we are richer or older or smarter or holier. Today.

This is not to suggest that we ignore the reality of our present circumstances in life; we are not playing some great game in which we boldly but blindly pretend that Bad is Good, that pain is pleasure. Instead we are challenged to see every moment, starting right now, as an opportunity to encounter the divine reality. If we define "Paradise" as the place where Jesus is, it only makes sense that we can experience something of heaven right here on earth, once we can see him alive and amongst us. His invitation, first expressed to a dying criminal, deserves an answer; perhaps we hardly dare to believe in its simplicity. We think that Paradise belongs to other people who are better than us and to another time that is still far off in the future. Jesus' words suggest that we take another look at today.

Lord, many of us already know what hell is like because we have vainly tried to live without your presence. Regardless of the circumstances of our lives—our health, our possessions—it is truly hell when we foolishly close ourselves off from you. You stand there, always ready to open the door to something better, yet many of us are too shy, too proud, too fearful, to follow you. Help me to see the reality of your Kingdom as it has already started to unfold around me.

27

The women
who did not run away

Mark 15:40-41

Courage has many forms. There is the courage of the warrior, trumpeted forth with brass bands and boastfulness, enhanced by epic sagas of strength, power and pride. This is a courage that loves to flex its muscles and roar occasionally, and the world sometimes needs to hear its forthright (but rarely humble) shouts of triumph. Another type of courage is easily hidden from public view, one that belongs to those who display none of the trappings of bravery—no powerful weapons, no revolutionary dreams, no idolizing legends or traditions of victory. This is the courage of the women who stood there on Calvary, looking on from a distance and waiting. We have recorded the names of the disciples in the glorious annals of sainthood, but while they continued to cower somewhere in fear, the women who followed

Jesus, most of them nameless and long forgotten, stood and kept vigil near the cross.

This is the courage of endurance: endurance of the pain that women have learned to accept as part of the rhythm of female life; endurance of the sweat and blood that must accompany the bliss of childbirth; endurance of the sacrifice that can always be found wherever love is. Watching little ones suffer through childhood illnesses for which there is no comfort or cure; waiting for husbands, brothers and sons to return from dangerous missions and uncharted voyages; following a leader who has come to an ignoble and frightening end there on Calvary—this is what women have endured over the centuries, often with little reward or even recognition.

And there is the courage of failure: the failure that recognizes when defeat is inevitable, and still one must continue to live and remember; the failure that keeps faith alive when more sensible people have decided to give up; the failure that can still hope in spite of the experience of happiness tempered by grief, of death tangled up with life, of the future ever burdened by the past. This is a courage that transcends success; that does not need to feed on glowing reports of battles won or new worlds conquered; a courage that can be sustained almost forever on a meagre diet of trust and tenderness.

This is the courage of those who take risks because they have nothing much to lose: no status, no power, no money. The courage of those who are rarely recognized for their talents and gifts, who have never learned the subtle arts of self-promotion and have grown all too accustomed to standing somewhere in the background. The out-and-out boldness of those who have spent an entire lifetime always working for others, never thinking of themselves first. Those women who stood there waiting and watching were very special people, for their generosity permitted Jesus to leave behind his trade and livelihood during the years of his public ministry. Yet we have not held their lives up as a glowing example worthy of our praise and remembrance; we have not reflected wisely on their faith and hope and love.

They stood there in silence, or perhaps letting their voices rise in the traditional keening sounds of sorrow that can still be heard wherever there is mourning in the Middle East. They might have watched on other days at the sight of similar scenes of bloodshed and violence, and with their healing arts and traditional medicines brought a measure of relief to others who were wounded and ill. They knew how to offer love and comfort, but there on Calvary they could do nothing except watch and pray: they could bring no other tangible gift to the one who hung there in wretched misery.

No splendid churches have been built in honour of The Women Who Did Not Run Away; there are no special days dedicated to their memory on the official church calendars. We rarely remind ourselves of the existence of their silent and subtle courage. The witness of these women, whether we recognize it or not, surely did not pass unnoticed by One who could see and treasure their presence.

> Lord, the world is still a harsh and brutal home for many women; the stories of their courage and endurance fill me with terrible rage and sadness. Too often those with power have justified this oppression by calling on sacred tradition in order to resist change. Help those whose daily existence is scarred by misery and neglect simply because they are women.

28

Mary, the mother of Jesus

John 19:25b

We call her Mary, the Blessed Virgin, Our Lady. Her real name was Miriam of Nazareth, the widow of Joseph the carpenter. She was a middle-aged woman, dark hair streaked with grey, olive skin gently marked with the lines that come with the passage of time. The beauty of most Mediterranean women does not disappear with age; it merely changes and matures. Her clothes were unremarkable: a plain linen dress in the colours of the earth (stone, taupe, or sand), a shawl or hooded cloak loosely covering her head. For centuries, the world has tried to imagine her as she stood near the cross on Calvary, watching her son's final moments of life.

We know nothing of her features, but many have thought that her face would be touched by wisdom, with eyes reflecting the serenity of a lifetime passed in faith. It is easy to see her still moving with the assurance of youth, still strong after her life of

135

hard work and physical activity. All those years in Nazareth, her hands were kept busy carrying water, grinding wheat, mending, cooking, cleaning. She was never wealthy enough to afford the servants that the wives and mothers of prosperous merchants, land-owners, or government officials would take for granted. In fact, much of her time was claimed by very ordinary responsibilities that left her with little leisure or luxury.

The hours that she spent waiting and watching on Calvary were a contrast to the industrious activity that formed the background of many of her days, yet we readily imagine her standing beneath the cross, a picture of stillness. It requires no great gift of imagi-nation or poetic fancy to understand the grief that would have touched her every nerve; there is no special talent needed to conjure up the unique anguish that a mother feels when watching her children suffer, regardless of age, rank or condition. Rather, it takes a little effort to see anything but the stillness and the grief; the human person becomes lost in the conventions of sorrow and superhuman anguish. And the reality of Miriam, with all the richness of her experience, has been further distorted, for this special woman has almost disappeared completely beneath our devotions and reverence. We have created a barrier to her through the paintings, hymns and cathedrals dedicated to her name; we no

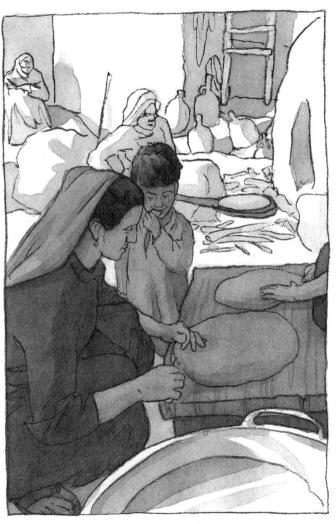

Mary at work

longer see a woman of flesh and blood, but only the reflections of a tradition that glorifies the saint but has hidden the human face.

And much of what we have enshrined in our art and devotions somehow does not belong to Miriam. We call her "meek and mild," forgetting the strength of her arms, arms that worked harder than many of us today ever will. We picture her lost in ethereal meditation, closing our eyes to the simplicity of her days there in Nazareth, days that involved conversations with neighbours, trips to the outdoor markets, visits with relatives, special events like weddings and festivals to punctuate each passing year. We let ourselves focus too intently on one or two aspects of her life—the suffering mother, the innocent maiden—according to our tastes and inclinations; we rarely let ourselves gather all our reflections about her into one, recognizable image of a human person. Our thoughts and prayers become sadly artificial, trapped inside the image of our favourite madonna, lulled to sleep by the echoes of a beloved hymn.

She stood there on Calvary, an aging woman who had memories of her child's first words, his first laugh, his first tentative steps. She brought with her to the cross the hopes and dreams that always seemed to be just out of reach; her pain would have been punctuated by thoughts that are easily recognizable to us: "We will never have another walk together. He will never tell me any more of his wonderful stories. I will never hear his voice again." If we let ourselves reflect on her timeless human experience of sadness and grief, faith and love, we may find that her voice still speaks clearly to us today.

Lord, I can only approach you through my humanity; I have to bring my whole person, with all its weaknesses and strengths, into every encounter with you. Sometimes we think that prayer has to involve some part of our selves that belongs to a world of spiritual perfection. Help me to speak to you with everything that is mine: body and soul, mind and strength.

29

"Woman, here is your son"

John 19:26-27

Artists for centuries have recognized that the form of a triangle is very pleasing to behold; whole compositions of elaborate complexity can be derived from this simple but powerful shape. In my parish church, the stained glass window over the altar is based on just such an arrangement of overlapping triangles. The theme of this carefully constructed window is the crucifixion; more specifically, the designer has chosen to include Jesus' mother and the beloved disciple standing at the foot of the cross. In effect, the window is a sensitive illustration of that touching bequest, "Woman, here is your son."

Circles, squares and triangles are the building blocks of all visual creation; a scholarly description of this stained glass window would explain that the two grieving figures on either side of the cross form the bottom edge of one triangle, establishing a sense of weight and solidity for the whole composition. And then there is the inverted triangle at the top of the design, its base formed by the outstretched arms of the cross. The whole work, simple and familiar as it may be, communicates a very powerful message; those interlocking triangles resonate with a very special harmony.

As we stand (or sit or kneel), looking up at any representation of the cross on Calvary, our hearts and minds can be moved by an almost overwhelming number of thoughts and impressions. Sometimes we are comforted by the recognition that Jesus' pain can be a mirror of our own experience; seen from another angle, the cross beckons us to reflect a little on the troubles of others who need our help. At another time, we forget about this world completely, lost in quiet contemplation of Jesus and his Kingdom. But regardless of the content of our reflections, there are only three possible starting places for all these thoughts and feelings. Each of us stands at one point of a triangle; on one side we can look outwards to Jesus, and on the other we can see the rest of the world. This three-sided relationship is simplicity itself, but it binds us as tightly as the strongest and most durable chain. Spiritual wisdom is rarely achieved from the perspective of selfish solitude; our prayers and meditations have little meaning if we are unable to see our neighbour somewhere on the other side.

Jesus, too, never forgot that he stood on this earth irrevocably linked to the concerns of all humanity. Food, shelter, warmth, clothing: throughout the Gospels, we have a witness to his interest in the simplest human values, starting with the physical well-being of those around him. And if we want to imitate his life and work, we are challenged to do so using the materials closest at hand. We desire affection and acceptance from our companions; we are drawn to places that are beautiful or inspiring; we need rest and recreation. The Christian heritage includes a healthy reverence for these ordinary human yearnings, because the simple gifts of life contain the image of a generous God who cares about every aspect of our existence. In the same way, we are asked to think about the most basic unit of human society, the family, just as Jesus thought of his mother and the beloved disciple during those sad final moments on Calvary.

Perhaps the word *family* no longer speaks to us of the comfort, acceptance and stability we remember from days gone by. We might consider instead that family is a word of such richness and depth that it can embrace a whole kaleidoscope of homes and relationships and associations. And just as we recognize that our friendship with God will depend on our treatment of others, so we begin to understand that there are a great many "others" who are joined to us on our journey through this life. The strangers lined up with us in the supermarket; the victims of an earthquake thousands of miles away; the passengers in the next car on the highway; the protesters at a rally on the other side of the world: these are the people who make up the one human family, linked to us because of the message of universal salvation that Jesus' life and death proclaimed. And just as we yearn to take comfort and consolation from his outstretched arms, so we are invited to open our homes to love; to bring comfort and care to those around us; to make a place within ourselves for affection and hope.

Lord, I wish that daily life could be more polite and serene; there always seems to be some new crisis, some new problem with time, money and space that prevents me from enjoying the company of all the strangers who surround me. Help me to find the patience and good humour to love this challenging human family.

30

"Darkness came over the whole land"

Mark 15:33

The modern world no longer fears the darkness, for we know that by turning a knob or pushing a button we can flood our rooms with light. Those in ages past were accustomed to the pale flickering light of candles and oil lamps; our ancestors would be dazzled by the brightness of our houses, the safety of our well-lit streets. We are able to turn night into day, prolonging our useful hours of work and recreation. No longer do we strain our eyes and our tempers, as students, seamstresses and scholars once did, trying to read or work or write in the inadequate light provided by the stump of a precious beeswax candle. And the light that we create is so powerful, so cheap, so readily accessible that our rooms are free from the gloomy and oppressive shades and shadows that we associate with the dimly lit halls and spooky old castles of Gothic romance. Some of us, thanks to underground pedestrian walkways and massive windowless offices, can pass whole days at work without ever seeing the sky; we are effectively divorced from the ancient limitations of hot and cold, darkness and light. The rhythms of nature no longer affect our patterns of activity.

Mark's description of the final hours before Jesus' death resonates with the fears and anxieties of a very different world: a world in which a natural phenomenon like weather was still poorly understood; a world in which the sun itself was worshipped as the source of all light and life; a world in which it was easy to be afraid of the darkness. Anthropologists have taught us that many societies once created complex rituals in order to placate the fickle gods of wind and rain; whole cultures worshipped the forces that rule the stars, the planets and, most of all, the sun. Until very recently, the image of a mysterious darkness coming over the earth at mid-day would send a shiver of fear through the hearts of even the brave; today we merely shrug and talk glibly about partial eclipses, sudden violent thunderstorms and poetic exaggeration.

Even if we disregard the physical sensation of darkness on the afternoon when Jesus died (and this is all too easy to do, sitting in a comfortable armchair with half a dozen electric lights somewhere close at hand), all of us can understand the darkness of spirit that came over Jesus' friends and companions in those last few hours. The disciples who were still off somewhere in hiding were experiencing a deep and depressing sense of loneliness, one compounded by guilt, regret and fear. One can imagine the oppressive sense of loss and emptiness that filled their thoughts and conversation wherever they hid. Those of Jesus' followers who remained with him experienced a different sense of loss after watching all that had transpired there on Calvary. The sight of the thorns, the nails and the cross would have drained the last remnants of strength from their tired and weary bodies.

We know what it means to watch a loved one struggling in a hospital bed for the last hour or two before death finally comes to still the laboured breathing; but as we watch, we sit in a clean, well-ordered space, surrounded by compassionate nurses and all the tools of modern medicine. Imagine instead those who watched on Calvary: standing out in the open, exhausted after a sleepless night, ignored by those who came to mock, unable to offer anything, not even a drink of cool water, to the one who suffered, and worst of all, deprived of any understanding of the true meaning of this death. This is a darkness as real as a winter night at the bottom of a bottomless pit, without moon or stars, without lamps or fire. The darkness of despair, sorrow, and fear. A darkness unrelieved by hope.

Life without Jesus represented life without hope both to those who stayed to watch and those who had run away. Life without Jesus is equally grim, equally without hope, for those of us today who are unable to hear anything besides empty piety in his words. We may continue to work and eat and sleep, successful in the eyes of the world, perhaps comfortable with the rhythm of our lives. Lost in the darkness, we will not even realize that somewhere there is Light.

> *Lord, many of us experience a profound darkness: the darkness of depression, despair and futility. Without a sustaining belief in you and your message of love and hope, the world can be a gloomy and threatening place indeed. Help me to let the light of your presence illuminate the hidden corners of my self, the dim and shadowy recesses where doubt and anxiety still live.*

31

"My God, my God,
why have you forsaken me?"

Mark 15:34

In a lifetime of encounters with the Mystery of God, there are inevitably a few painful moments that call forth a response of anger and despair. Usually, our time-honoured prayers and religious observances let us bury certain fears underneath a comfortable layer of ritual and tradition. Once in a while, however, an intense and unsettling event forces us to speak of a truth that we rarely care to examine, and then our words flash forth, fed by a fire long suppressed; only expressions of powerful, even brutal, honesty do justice to the shadow that lies hidden in our inner heart of hearts. We are driven to put aside the politeness and composure of conventional prayer in order to express that which we most dread: our experience of the absence of God.

Thanks to the customs of polite civilization, we rarely share these wrenching moments with the outside world, moments that are difficult to acknowledge even to ourselves. It is painful to expose the emptiness that lives somewhere in every human soul; any sincere experience of this truth is bound to leave us shaken and subdued. It requires honesty and courage to admit that there are times when we have to stand alone, when the pillars and supports of our faith, like some great celestial magic show, seem to have vanished from the stage.

Jesus' dying words shatter the silence of the centuries with the same ferocious power as those explosions of doubt and frenzy that still unnerve us today: "My God, my God, why have you forsaken me?" It is little consolation to realize that this cry from the heart of a dying man is also a quotation from one of the Psalms.[1] Knowing that these words of despair and longing belong to the great Hebrew and Christian scriptures, we are reminded that much of the agony of Calvary is not unique; there have been others who were also moved to cry out in a loud voice using this very same language.

The human race seems cursed to endure much that is painful to witness and dreadful to experience, but nothing is worse than the moments in which we feel utterly abandoned and alone. Cries of despair still echo through us today, and, like Jesus and the

---

[1]   Psalm 22.

psalmist before him, we are moved to call out to a God who seems to have forsaken all that belongs to this creation. We are desperate to hide our own emptiness, yet there is little solace in the pleasures and distractions of life; the business of existence, the care and feeding of body and mind, is not enough for fulfilment. We cry out for something more, and Nothing seems to come forth.

These are the times when the only experience we have of God is shrouded in doubt and ambiguity. Here we stand, created in the image and likeness of Someone who has suddenly become deaf to our prayers and blind to our needs. We gaze across the vast desert of human despair, the wasteland of broken dreams and bitter memories, and we wonder where God is through all of this. Could it be that our creator is no longer interested? Is our universe nothing more than a gigantic clockwork toy, set in motion at the beginning of time by a bored and restless inventor who has now moved on to better things, leaving us alone to fend miserably for ourselves? Is it possible that the God of Goodness is merely a figment of our weak-willed imaginations, something we invoke to comfort the childishly immature elements in our nature? And try as we might, however strong we claim our faith to be, however much we think we may know about the intricacies of philosophy and theology, no one is immune to this experience of God's absence.

"My God, my God," we want to cry out, "why have you forsaken us, leaving behind a world where boredom and frustration are endemic, where we are forever called upon to witness the suffering of ourselves and others? The chronicle of human misery: the senseless accidents, the horrendous natural disasters, the insane ravages of war: we see all these realities. Do you? You who are supposed to be Love itself, where are you?" And sometimes we hear no answer to that prayer.

> Lord, I too have cried out in a hollow angry voice because so much of life appears to be useless, incomprehensible, futile. Without some faith in you, human existence with all its suffering must seem meaningless. Help me to find the courage to trust you, even when I cannot understand.

32

"I am thirsty"

John 19:28

With a phrase that is deceptively simple, John's Gospel describes the emptiness of Jesus' last moments: "I am thirsty." Each of the four Gospel narratives includes some mention of the reed soaked in vinegar and offered to the dying man, testimony to the ancient tradition surrounding this episode. We who read these words today have many different places from which to begin our reflections.

Children in their innocence come upon this detail of the Passion story and immediately focus on the most obvious aspect: plain, ordinary thirst. The young, after all, are far more aware of their simple bodily needs than those of us trained by time to be patient and self-controlled. They also recognize that Jesus' words have been repeated by everyone, themselves included, over and over again. But this simple explanation, poignant and universally understood as it may be, also has its limitations, for there is much more that should be said about thirst.

When confronted by these words in John's Gospel, a medical expert might begin a discussion of the raging thirst which follows any severe loss of blood. Those who understand the workings of the human body have often studied the Gospel accounts in the light of Roman crucifixion practice and, thus informed, they can talk about this thirst as an entirely believable reaction to the suffering described by the evangelists. Their comments are correct, of course, but the simple words, "I thirst," also speak about something that transcends mere physical suffering.

Psychologists would comment on this episode from an entirely different perspective, reflecting on that great universal thirst: the quest for self-esteem, approval and fulfilment. They would examine the persistent questions that have inspired many to search for some fountain of enlightenment; they would recognize the ways in which Jesus' thirst mirrors the dryness of disillusionment that afflicts so many. Yet, even these insights into the needs of the human person do not include anything of the great spiritual longing also implied by this simple phrase.

Scripture scholars who come upon this little section are reminded of similar incidents elsewhere in the Bible; they enthusiastically seize upon these other related passages, especially the psalm that refers to

154

"If you thirst . . ."

vinegar offered insultingly as drink.[1] Much would be made of all the Biblical images of water, altogether appropriate in a semi-arid land that treasured every stream and river and well. Finally, all this study would be connected to Jesus' description of himself as the living water, now contrasted to the perception that he would have to drain a bitter cup before he died. And however profound the scholars' analyses might be, they too would not have exhausted all the possibilities.

The student of literature takes the words "I am thirsty," and like the child, notices that this is a phrase of the utmost simplicity and directness. Going beyond the child's understanding of basic human needs, those who love words for their own sake also mark the contrast between this ordinary sentence and the richness and eloquence found elsewhere in Jesus' life, the parables, his farewell discourses, the great sermons. And from the perspective of poetry, it is a sobering experience to observe a dying man stripped of the beloved arts of rhetoric and left with only the very simplest of simple sentences.

Whenever we look at any aspect of the Passion story, each of us is like this chorus of observers, at one time obsessed by the most literal interpretation of the facts, at another inspired by hidden metaphorical

---

[1]   Psalm 69:21.

meanings; on one day, we are swept away into flights of poetic fancy, on another we are brought back to earth by the naive and uncomplicated child within. It is an act of courage to admit that the truth of the simple words of the Gospels cannot be unravelled in a few sentences, or reduced to the certainty of a mathematical formula. Without the dimension of faith and prayer, the story of Jesus' life and death is little more than an interesting historical romance from long ago and far away.

Lord, I am thirsty too, and sometimes I do not know what I need to drink. Experts tell us that we need many things: comfort, knowledge, understanding, endurance. There is much that is still unfinished in my life; help me to accept that I must ask in order to receive.

33

"Into your hands
I commend my spirit"

Luke 23:46

The words of the dying are always held in a certain reverence. We who remain behind listen with grave concentration, as if something of the mystery of death were hovering there beside us, ready to whisper some secret message of hope into our expectant ears. Jesus' last words as reported in Luke's Gospel are a quotation from one of the Psalms;[1] Luke's special sense of the dramatic combines with his profound spirituality to create this quiet moment of peace at the end of the Passion story.

The Psalm quoted by Jesus was not composed specifically for a scene of death; it is a lament of David that recounts the life and struggles of one who has been wrongfully oppressed. Its imagery belongs to the everyday world of flesh and bone; it calls out to a

---

[1]   Psalm 31:5.

God of physical power and might, one capable of rescuing the speaker from the real human sufferings that are described so warmly in its vivid Hebrew poetry. And it is to the living that Luke is writing his elegant, literate Greek prose, to Christians like you and me, who are sometimes put upon a cross of suffering, a cross often created by our own folly and neglect. We are invited to enter the serenity of Jesus' last few moments, not because we yearn to be released into a heaven of unimaginable bliss, but because the hell of this present world comes with us whenever we encounter our Eternal Creator.

There comes a time when each of us will know what it means to kneel beside that rock in the garden, and look at the bitter cup that is waiting for us. We remember the blows that have been inflicted upon our battered souls, and we wonder if any of the cuts and bruises will ever begin to heal. We have to pick up our cross every day, willingly or unwillingly, however much we resent its weight; and we know all too well that we will stumble and fall along the way. But unless we arrive with Jesus at the moment when we finally let his peace overcome us, surrendering ourselves and our struggles into Someone Else's hands, our suffering is as the suffering of a dumb animal: pathetic, not poignant; futile, not meaningful; full of the waste of destruction, and far removed from the still, silent beauty of sacrifice.

Can we learn to pray like Jesus, using words and phrases that remind us, moment after moment, that it is this present pain and this present problem that need to be carried to the foot of our own personal Calvary? Or are we trapped behind a wall of pride that surely does nothing to lessen the weight of our cross, and prevents us from acknowledging our own most humble needs? Oh, how arrogance and vanity can create a barrier thicker and stronger than anything built by mere science and technology! Add in a little deep-seated shame to make us more reluctant to face the truth of our burdens, and eventually we will find ourselves looking with curious indifference at a cross that never leaves some dusty museum of religious artifacts. We will listen to Jesus' dying words and think of nothing more than those clever anthologies that immortalize the deathbed thoughts of other famous thinkers. Without some trust in the power of the cross, there is nothing here to catch hold of us in our deepest personal struggles, to transform the dull, chronic pain of the human condition into something liberating and free.

The redemption that took root in the soil of Calvary, watered by the blood, sweat and tears of One like us, does not promise a world without pain and struggle. It is a promise for those who already know the meaning of uncertainty and disappointment; for those who have looked in the mirror and seen Failure staring back; for those who have the strength to face up to their own weakness. It is a message addressed to everyone who once tried to take up that cross alone, ready at last to accept a little help.

> *Lord, I cannot find serenity anywhere; like a bird caught in a net, the more I struggle, the less I am able to break free. To bring my restless heart into the light of your presence requires such a leap of faith and hope; help me to open myself to your love so that I can at last be at peace.*

34

"It is finished"

After his hours of physical and mental suffering, there came a moment when Jesus, like many others on the verge of death, acknowledged that his life was coming to an end. We often turn our mind's eye towards the twisted figure on the cross, but from the distance of centuries it is difficult to see the whole picture. We watch Jesus alive and still suffering, or we imagine him already in death, lifeless, pale and cold. Those who stood at the foot of the cross were a witness to something else: the transition that fills any who watch with reverence and awe. John's Gospel commemorates an experience that is waiting for all of us.

Those who are dying approach the doorway of death with warm blood still flowing through veins and arteries; some small hints of activity—the flicker of an eyelid, a movement in the line of the mouth—are proof that life yet endures. As energy slowly drains away from the human frame, there comes one final moment when an irreversible transformation takes place. The body's functions start to fail until at last it is no longer possible to draw another breath; the heart stops beating and life is over. As death arrives, some sense of relaxation and tranquillity returns, a look of contentment, a quiet smile; there is no further strain or effort, no laboured breathing, no random or erratic movements. If there are wounds, the blood stops trickling, and those there present know that it is finished. The body has slowly arrived at the final state of rest that can be such a comfort to those who watch, for the struggle and discomfort of suffering fade away, and everything is transformed into the silence and peace of quiet sleep. But whatever stillness is visible on the surface, inside there are further changes, for the soul remains on a voyage, with a destination that is not entirely possible to describe or explain.

"It is finished," we read in the words of John's Gospel; long before these words were written, those who watched observed it to be so. And with the same conflicting emotions that trouble us when we keep vigil at a deathbed, those at the foot of the cross were grateful that Jesus' sufferings had finally come to an end. At the same time they felt in themselves the sadness and even despair of their own bereavement. We who listen to these words in church on Good

Friday, or read them at home in our own Bibles, bow our heads in reverence, but we do not sink down in devastation as those who watched might well have done when that final moment came. We read, "It is finished," and we reflect instead on completeness, redemption, fulfilment. We do not think about a tomorrow morning that will dawn empty because of the absence of our friend, or son, or teacher.

Instead, we watch Jesus in death, and our faith tells us to wait for tomorrow in a spirit of hope and even excitement; we learn to say prayers and sing hymns in the face of his departure because we have already recognized him as the One who conquered death itself. We cannot repress that liberating experience of the risen Lord; whenever we are confronted by other events as troubling as that first Good Friday, we have been taught to remind ourselves that the ending there on Calvary was really a new beginning. And our own most private fears are soothed because of what we believe.

Nevertheless, in spite of our faith and the comfort that it is supposed to offer, we sometimes feel more like those who watched by the cross, ignorant of the ultimate meaning of this death. The world around us still lives in terror of extinction, with a primitive and contagious fear of death and sickness; we are hard pressed sometimes to explain "redemption" to those who reject the values of Jesus' life, let alone the horror of his death. For those who try to survive without any faith in a loving Providence, life is a series of inexplicable accidents, a random mixture of pleasure and pain, and suffering is something to be avoided at all cost. It is a challenge to those of us who think otherwise to refute that view. We have been left here to proclaim our belief in redemption, using nothing more than the witness of our ordinary days, days of sickness and health, success and disappointment, life and death.

> *Lord, it is too easy to think that life stretches on forever when we are occupied with the activities of a busy life; I sometimes forget that there is a limit to the time allotted for the length of my days. I try to pretend that there are an endless number of tomorrows waiting for me. Help me to remember that, one day, I too will have to say, "It is finished."*

35

"The curtain of the temple was torn in two"

Mark 15:38

In the book of Exodus, we read about the first sanctuary which the Israelites built at Yahweh's command, a symbol of the Lord's presence amongst his people. Included in this revered place of worship was to be a finely woven curtain, rich with splendid embroideries of angelic cherubim, designed to separate the outer tabernacle from the innermost Holy of Holies. In both the Old and New Testaments, there are many references to other precious treasures belonging to the magnificent Temple built later on by Solomon in Jerusalem: the golden altar of incense, the many-branched candelabra, the Ark of the Covenant. From these details, we can conjure up the memory of a sacred dwelling held in the highest esteem by a whole nation, one in which the most important and moving rituals took place.

More importantly, we know that the innermost Holy of Holies, hidden behind that richly elaborate curtain, could not be approached by everyone; in those days, only the high priest had direct access to the most sacred Presence dwelling therein. Mark, Matthew and Luke include the destruction of this curtain in their accounts of the Passion story, a dramatic climax appropriate to a scene of sudden and violent death. And the destruction of this curtain, powerfully symbolic and mystically beautiful as it is, conveys a very important image: the image of a new covenant brought about by Jesus' death, a new relationship between the ordinary people of this world and God Almighty. The symbolism of the torn curtain is entirely consistent with all that we know of the life of Jesus, for he came to teach us that any possible boundary between ourselves and our Creator has now been removed. His liberation of the world— the dismantling of every artificial barrier based on race or sex or position—was as much a part of his message as the great commandments of love and service.

There are many different invitations issued throughout the Gospels; on page after page we are called to experience love, generosity and forgiveness. The symbol of the destruction of the curtain is yet another of these invitations. Perhaps we lose sight of this because we are distracted by all the confusing historical details about the famous Temple in Jerusalem during the different eras of Judaism. Or we dismiss the incident as one more example of the love of miracles and superstition in the ancient world. And since the very word *curtain* reminds us of nothing more than a scrap of flimsy lace at a dusty parlour window—and not an impressive tapestry guarding the God of our ancestors—we miss a truly important symbol: the long-closed door finally flung open for all the world to enter.

We are now free to walk through that door into a holy place once reserved for a priestly elite; hand in hand with that freedom come challenges and opportunities. Each of us now has a responsibility towards the duties that once belonged exclusively to the hereditary leaders of the old religion. And as our whole society becomes more educated and independent, the traditional distinction between the official ministers of religion and the ordinary lay person continues to evolve. However we interpret the command to proclaim the Gospel, we recognize that we can no longer leave that task exclusively to one distinct segment of society; each of us as a Christian has been singled out to preach the life and death of Jesus.

The royal priesthood that we read about in the First Letter of Peter[1] has been entrusted to you and

---

[1] 1 Peter 1:9.

me and every other person sitting there in the pews on a Sunday morning. How sadly disappointing that such a wondrous vocation is limited in many of our imaginations to an hour of worship per week! Most of life takes place somewhere else: in homes, offices, schools, restaurants, shopping centres. The thousands of hours that we spend doing ordinary "secular" things give us abundant opportunity to proclaim the Good News. We have been invited into the Holy of Holies to encounter God in the most direct way possible, and then to take our knowledge and experience back into the world.

> *Lord, sometimes we get angry (maybe rightly so) at the official hierarchy of our religion. It is much easier to blame the institutional church for its lapses than to take upon ourselves the responsibility for proclaiming your message in our lives. You have invited me to share my faith with the world around me; help me to have the courage to do so, regardless of the actions and attitudes of our leaders.*

36

The centurion speaks

Mark 15:39

The centurion stood there for hours, bored and restless, watching the sky for rain, hoping everything would be over before nightfall. With indifference he heard the sound of nails being hammered through flesh and bone; he hardly noticed the little rivulets of blood trickling down into a pool at the foot of the cross. He had witnessed this scene and worse many times before; anyone in command of one hundred Roman soldiers knew all about cruelty and violence. The centurions were usually from ordinary families, plebeians not patricians,[1] having been promoted through the ranks of the regular army. Once upon a time, this centurion had seen duty as a humble foot soldier, starting off on the muddy tracks of Gaul or the dusty roads of Spain on the way to this commission in far-off Judea. Now he was immune to

---

1   Roman aristocrats.

emotional storms and nervous reactions, accustomed to the hardships of life in one of the turbulent outposts of the Empire. He did not stand there on Calvary expecting to see visions and miracles.

Nevertheless, Mark's Gospel tells us that he did, as if a Reality above and beyond the physical dimension of the cross had called out to him during those tedious hours of watching. And for one brief moment, we who reflect on this scene hear something besides the mocking voice of the crowd, the low moans of the two bandits, the muffled laments of grieving friends. In the presence of that pale and lifeless body hanging there in death, the centurion spoke about something that the world had waited for centuries to see: "Truly this man was God's son."

These few words stand as testimony to an event and a person and a truth that was unique in all human history. The prophets, patriarchs and anointed rulers of Israel had heard nothing like this during their long days of waiting for a Messiah. Through all those years of anticipation, the prayers of the righteous were addressed to a far-off God whose face always remained partially hidden, even from those steeped in holiness and virtue. Here on Calvary, one who did not share that heritage looked at the cross and saw something that turned scorn into belief. The centurion broke through a barrier with his words of faith and hope. He spoke for all those who waited; he spoke to us.

The centurion of Mark's Gospel did not try to understand all the reasons why a Son of God might be found hanging there on Calvary in the company of common criminals. He did not investigate all the layers of meaning that resonate through words like "sacrifice," "redemption" and "salvation." He merely spoke one quiet and truthful sentence; the world has reflected ever since on some of the other implications of Jesus' life and death. Many questions remain unanswered, questions to which we often respond in frustrated silence. What kind of Messiah is found in such a place? What kind of faith needs these repeated images of blood and degradation? What kind of Father wants this sacrifice from his Son?

The struggle to answer these questions is a challenge to even the sincerest believer. Furthermore, not every attempt to clarify and explain this mystery of faith has been successful. Too often in the past, those called upon to speak in the name of Jesus' family have interpreted the events on Calvary using harsh words and frightening images, in a misguided effort to convince the world of the wickedness of human ways. Here is the perfect tool to remind us of the wretchedness of our behaviour! As a result, the cross has become a symbol of repentance rooted in fear, and not a reminder of sacrifice inspired by love.

Those who are honest in their search for wisdom recognize that mere words are never enough to explain the meaning of Calvary; a Power beyond human experience remains there, an eternal Reality outside the limits of human comprehension. Only when we give ourselves over to the force of God's love can we begin to understand the voice that spoke so clearly on that day long ago, a voice that carried with it some of the sanctity and beauty of that pale wounded body. Like the centurion, we too will learn to speak about a Son who chose to suffer in the presence of his almighty Father, the Parent who rejoices in the self-sacrificing love of this faithful Child.

> Lord, there comes a time when it is no longer possible to keep silent. We may be inspired to speak out against an injustice long felt; we may be moved to express our belief in your loving presence in words that are a contrast to the superficial conversation of every day. Help me to use my voice to celebrate your truth; help me to find the right words to say.

37

His side was pierced with a lance

John 19:31-37

The sky was nearly dark, the clouds darker still; it was almost nightfall and the soldiers standing guard on Calvary were heartily sick of this place. Any minute now it might start raining; those storm clouds looked ready to burst. Thunder rumbled in the distance, lightning flashed across the far horizon. Most of the sightseers had departed long ago for the welcome shelter of home; only the morbidly curious and a few overwrought mourners were left here on the hill. The two thieves were nearly gone, already unconscious; in a few minutes more they would be put out of their misery. The man in the middle who hardly looked like a criminal, the one they laughingly called a King, his life was definitely over. Still, they had to make sure: one can never tell in this half-light of early evening; sometimes the unlucky ones lingered on for days. So one of the soldiers took up his lance and pierced the body in the side; a little blood came out, then water. There was nothing left of the King after all.

The soldiers prepared to head back to Jerusalem, glad to return to whatever inn or barracks they called home, looking forward to food, a little wine, perhaps some fun and games in the taverns after this long boring day. The street kids in Rome thought it was exciting to be in the legions; if they only knew! Sentry duty at these godforsaken execution sites was the worst job of all; the crowds of excitable relatives and friends, some shouting and screaming; weeping women falling down and fainting; impossible to keep any kind of order here. Once in a while the mob even threw rocks. The ever-alert spectators might try to sneak off with the slim pickings that were every soldier's due, the few decent clothes they might scrounge if there was anything worth taking. At last this day was finally over. There was no point in lingering behind once the centurion gave his sign that their business was done; no one bothered to take a second look at the tableau of crosses etched against the sky in the dying daylight. If the centurion had doubts about this afternoon's work, that was his problem. They were not judges; they were just there to carry out orders.

Only the few faithful friends who had also stood there all day long remained; they could hardly recognize the features of their loved one under the blood and the dirt. But they remembered him all the same: the Leader who welcomed his companions for dinner, who was never at a loss for words in his disputes with the Pharisees, who could captivate enormous outdoor crowds with his moral vision and heartfelt parables: and their grief swelled up again. These poor friends shuddered when the soldier stood there with his lance, and the blood and water flowed from his side: one more indignity offered to his body, one more gratuitous act of violence, pointless and insulting.

Today we still stand and "look on one who had been pierced" but we see in this event a symbol of the new covenant forged in the blood of the cross and the cleansing waters of baptism. The soldier's lance for us is one of the traditional instruments of the Passion, the gash in Jesus' side one of his five wounds. We too may recoil from the violence, but we know that it was not pointless. We reflect on the indignities; they give us strength to cope with our own struggles. We see the blood and the water, and however much we may regret our past mistakes, we know that this new covenant gives us hope for a better future. Like those who stood on Calvary during those final moments, we too remember the Teacher who belonged to the human world of first-century Palestine. We also see the cross and its timeless burden of sacrifice, and we have found a way to make sense of this suffering. Someone who is the bridge between human weakness and eternal perfection has shown us the way—a way rich with promise for those who believe. And we wait with renewed hope for the arrival of Easter.

Lord, it's a long time since I was baptized; many things have happened to me since, some wonderful, some that I'd rather not remember. When I look up to you on the cross, help me to see not just your death, but also your promise of new life, the same new life that belongs to me through baptism.

38

Joseph of Arimathea

Mark 15:42-43

The figure of Joseph of Arimathea quietly entered the stage at the very end of the Passion story. He offered to bury Jesus' body in his own empty tomb; in those days there were many gravesites hewn out of limestone rock in the outlying districts around Jerusalem. It was already dark when he approached Pilate with his request for permission to proceed with the burial. Darkness was no great problem since the simple Jewish funeral preparations involved little more than spices, ointments and clean linen cloths. On the other hand, boldly claiming the body of an executed criminal required either the bravery of strong conviction or the protection of wealth and social position. It is therefore no surprise that the Gospels described Joseph as either a rich and respected member of the council or as a secret follower of Jesus.

The four evangelists tell us very little else about this person; it is only in later centuries that his figure assumed its gigantic profile, for legend has it that Joseph of Arimathea was responsible for bringing the Holy Grail away from Jerusalem. Those who know the great romances of King Arthur and his knights and ladies, in any of their many and varied forms, are familiar with this other Joseph. Whether we think of the fabled city of Camelot, the richly symbolic poetry of Tennyson and T. S. Eliot, or Wagner's opera *Parsifal*, the quest for the mythical Holy Grail has been linked for a thousand years to the biblical figure of Joseph of Arimathea. And the idea of the Grail— the cup used at the Last Supper is only one of its possible descriptions—has tantalized many who search for riches, spiritual or otherwise.

After the events of the first Easter, the spread of the Good News of Jesus' life, death and resurrection was to be rapid and worldwide; we who still heed this message today are living proof of its power to take root in wildly differing cultures and historical settings. And regardless of the later career of Joseph of Arimathea, there has been much more to that message than magic relics and supernatural revelations. The belief in Jesus who is the Way between this human, imperfect life and the eternal peace of God has proven to be something that has liberated millions and millions of people from their own anxieties and struggles, spiritual and temporal. Countless parables and lessons from the pages of the New Testament have brought reassurance to the lonely, comfort to the sick, and consolation to those who mourn. This in itself is something of a miracle.

All of which brings us back to Joseph of Arimathea and the legendary adventures of those who eventually followed in his footsteps. It is ironic that the Holy Grail, chalice of immeasurable mystery and power, was always described in the most exclusive and elitist terms possible. Originally a simple pottery cup belonging on the supper table of an ordinary family in Palestine, the Grail was turned into a bejewelled chalice of the greatest imaginable worth. Only someone of the purest virtue could see it; all others were destined to waste a thousand lifetimes in their brave and courageous search, all to no avail. The Holy Grail of legend belongs to a world of larger-than-life heroes; it bears little resemblance to the real legacy of Jesus' life.

For if there is one thing upon which all Christians agree, it is the universal power of Jesus' message, his ability to reach out to everyone—not just the heroic and the beautiful—who came his way. The Gospel stories tell us more than once, in the plainest, most unmistakable terms, that Jesus came specifically to call those who were all too aware of their own faults. He didn't demand any proof of virtuous living and heroic deeds; he asked only for Faith. And Faith allows us to open ourselves to his power, something far more potent than any relic the world can ever imagine, and to let that power change us. And if we are already perfect, we have no need of the Christ who died on Calvary and was buried in a borrowed tomb. It doesn't require an enormous amount of humility to recognize that none of us has yet reached that stage of complete perfection that the poets ascribed to Sir Galahad, the only knight who was granted the privilege of seeing the fabulous Holy Grail. Perhaps we can rejoice instead in our unfinished humanity that leads us to accept the help of One who knew what it was to suffer and die just like us.

> *Lord, most of us are not heroes; our lives are not distinguished by noble quests and inspiring adventures. We don't always behave like saints either. Help me to remember that you came to save everyone, especially those whom the world calls sinners.*

39

Mary Magdalene

Mark 15:40, 47

She was present at three of the most important scenes of the Passion story: she saw Jesus die on Calvary; she witnessed his burial in the cave hewn out of the rock; she returned to the tomb on Sunday morning and experienced for herself the message of Easter. One scriptural commentary describes her as "the principle of continuity"; her presence at these three crucial times is mentioned in all four Gospels. Unfortunately, there is little more recorded about this important disciple, Mary Magdalene.

Later tradition took the figure of Mary of Magdala, a woman of courage and devotion, and identified her with another equally courageous and devoted person: the woman whose great sins were forgiven.[1] Perhaps this identification started because both women are seen carrying fragrant oils and

---

[1]   See Luke 7:36-50, and others.

precious spices to anoint the body of Jesus, one in life and the other in death. The Mary Magdalene of the art world is always portrayed with immense quantities of long, flowing hair, in remembrance of that other woman who passionately washed Jesus' feet with her tears and dried them with her hair. She has become a poignant symbol of penitence, the reformed sinner whose public gesture of love and faith touched Jesus during his dinner at the Pharisee's house; there is only a little scriptural evidence to suggest that these two women were really one and the same. But regardless of the gaps in our knowledge about her, Mary Magdalene was obviously a special person in Jesus' life.

It is sometimes difficult to realize that Jesus had friends, not just disciples who followed him as a Master is followed by his servants, but friends like Mary Magdalene who rejoiced in his ordinary human presence. At the same time, however much these followers celebrated his human qualities, they eventually understood that Jesus had a claim on them beyond the ordinary human obligations of loyalty and affection. During his life they sensed that he was much more than any friend could ever be. They began to address him in words that traditionally belonged only to God; they were preparing themselves to follow him into places outside the boundary of ordinary human experience. All those who followed Jesus during his time on earth, offering both worship and love, are models for us who come so many years later, for we too have learned to call him brother and friend, Lord and God.

At some point on our journey to Calvary, we also realize that Jesus is someone unique in all human history, someone who combines divine power and goodness with a human existence capable of suffering and death. This understanding of Jesus' nature has challenged believers for centuries; councils draft proclamations, theologians fight one another and historians write monographs, all because it takes a huge leap of faith to look at this person and see the human and the divine together there in one face. Can we ever explain this mystery? The Gospels contain important stories to remind us of his humanity, but no pen can fully express all that rightly belongs to the One we call Messiah, Christ, Emmanuel. No description of signs and wonders can convert us to his side; no creeds or edicts can force this belief. We have to wait, like Mary Magdalene and the other disciples, to experience his living presence for ourselves.

Mark looked back over the life and death of Jesus from the perspective of Easter; we who read his narrative today are told right from the first sentence that we are going to hear good news. The picture of Mary Magdalene—a distraught woman standing first at a public execution place and then in a vast cemetery on the outskirts of a city—is not exactly "good news." Similarly, if all we see of Jesus is the human face, the engaging philosopher, the charismatic leader, his story too has no happy ending. When we turn the page to the next chapter and find Mary Magdalene back at the empty tomb very early on the first day of the week, then we can understand the words of the evangelist. Those who watched the sufferings of Calvary are also privileged to witness the triumph of their friend, once dead and now the conqueror of death.

Lord, it is difficult to remember the actions of your life, the sufferings of your death, and the victory of your resurrection all at once. I get too involved in my reflections about one side of your story and forget about the two other dimensions to your good news. Help me to stretch my heart and my mind to experience your message more completely.

40

Jesus is laid in the tomb

Mark 15:46

We have been on a long journey, starting in a quiet garden on a hillside, winding through the old cobbled streets of Jerusalem, finally arriving at the desolation of The Place of the Skull. This has not been a pleasant holiday excursion, a light-hearted trip through scenic countryside, an amusing distraction from work and family responsibilities. Instead, there has been much on this road to challenge us, to make us think, to help us pray. In this final scene, however, we can at last put aside the troubling details of suffering and death; the violence and bloodshed are now over. It is time to move down from the hill of Calvary to stand in the silence of the Jerusalem cemetery.

It was already late on Friday evening when Jesus' body was wrapped in a plain linen cloth and placed in the tomb provided by Joseph of Arimathea. Only a few friends stood there in the cool night air;

we can imagine their exhaustion and grief. And just as Jesus' birth had once been celebrated in poverty and obscurity, so he was buried with quiet simplicity. No long and impressive funeral cortège proclaimed to the watching world that he had been honoured and loved in his lifetime. The officials who had ordered the crucifixion planned to forget about this burial as quickly as possible; this tomb seemed destined to be lost in totally deserved oblivion forever.

Eventually the moment came when those who watched the simple burial had to walk back to their homes in the darkened city. Those few faithful followers found little to comfort them there; perhaps they took refuge in the simplest of domestic duties: lighting the wick of an oil lamp, putting a dish of olives and bread on the table, washing their hands with cool water from an earthenware pitcher. They expected tomorrow to dawn empty, cold and lonely; despair and fear hung over those who mourned.

We too have stood by the graves of our loved ones, reluctant to return to the waiting world, but as we dry our eyes and prepare to face the business of life again, we are often advised to leave grief behind us. We reflect on the words found in countless funeral orations and graveside homilies—"I am the Resurrection and the Life"—and we are comforted. As we say good-bye, we remind ourselves that death is not the end; for those whom we mourn, it is only the beginning. The long journey to Calvary and beyond changed the meaning of death forever.

And the events of Calvary and beyond changed the meaning of life forever. It is not just those who have died and gone to their rest who can begin to share in the Resurrection and the Life that Jesus promised. We too, right here and now, are invited to experience some of the tremendous rebirth that was trumpeted forth on the first Easter Sunday. The One who first conquered death has promised to be with us today, while we are still tied to all that is limited, frail and incomplete in this wounded world. Jesus may have suffered and died on Calvary, but the great messages of his life have not been lost to death.

Nevertheless, like those who stood at the grave-side in Jerusalem, we still have moments that are empty of joy and peace and purpose. After all, we are not perfect yet! But every time we consciously turn our thoughts away from ourselves, looking with even the smallest amount of trust towards the person of Jesus, we find that something truly liberating does happen. Our journey takes on a new meaning. The faith upon which all human life depends grows deeper and more secure; somewhere we find the strength within to leave our problems and faults behind, to start over again afresh. Hope begins to take shape where once there had been little more than empty longing; we can watch the suffering of

Calvary and still be comforted, at rest in Jesus' peace. And a little spark of love catches fire, igniting all that is best within ourselves, our joy, our enthusiasm, our courage, and we begin to change. Every day can be another Easter. We are no longer like those who stood by the tomb on Good Friday night, forlorn, confused, overcome by the exhaustion of despair; we are like those who heard the Good News on Easter Sunday morning.

> Lord, to change this world, you had to suffer and die, and eventually be laid to rest in a tomb. And in spite of the Easter message, there still remains much that needs to be healed and renewed in this world. As I continue the journey of my life, help me to remember that you were not lost to death. Help me to remember that you give all that is best in me a chance to blossom and grow.

Epilogue

After the days of rain and thunder, threatening skies and gloomy faces, Sunday finally arrived with clear prospects and the promise of a beautiful day. Very early in the morning, as moon and stars faded and the sky turned from black to midnight blue, a few tired wayfarers appeared on the sleeping city streets. Their footsteps led them in the direction of the vast cemetery on the outskirts of Jerusalem; they brought with them jars of spices, linen cloths and heavy hearts.

Only those who travel abroad at this early hour are privileged to watch the full glory of a spring sunrise: the streaks of cream and lilac spreading across the Eastern heavens; the first rosy blush on the clouds at dawn. There was music too in the fresh morning air: the wind breathing softly through the leaves of the poplar trees; larks and swallows chanting springtime hymns of new life and new growth; water laughing and singing over the shiny pebbles of a nearby stream. Meanwhile, the sun continued its journey, now splashing red and gold over the horizon, its rays growing stronger and stronger, flooding earth and sky with light and warmth.

The burden of our travellers suddenly became lighter to carry. They looked up to the sky, entered the cemetery, and heard the good news. This was not how they expected the morning to begin!